Don Tippie
Eph 6:23

Liure Tippie
Col. 3:12-14

HE SAID,
SHE SAID,
GOD SAID

BIBLICAL ANSWERS
TO MARRIAGE QUESTIONS

DAN AND GINA TRIPPIE

CROSSBOOKS
PUBLISHING

CrossBooks™
A Division of LifeWay
1663 Liberty Drive
Bloomington, IN 47403
www.crossbooks.com
Phone: 1-866-879-0502

Cover Design and Interior Graphics: Typework Studio
Author Photo: Julie Marie Photography
Edited by: Michael Lukasik

First published by CrossBooks   12/17/13

ISBN: 978-1-4627-3388-0 (sc)
ISBN: 978-1-4627-3389-7 (e)

Printed in the United States of America.

This book is printed on acid-free paper.

Praise for
He Said, She Said, God Said

He Said, She Said, God Said is a great book on the fundamental truths of marriage written by a couple who have walked these principles out in their own lives. If you are interested in marriage or have been married for any period of time, this book will be of great encouragement to you as it helps explain God's desire for marriage. First, it focuses on the biblical ideal for marriage. Second, it's written by a couple who have given their lives to discover what those biblical principles mean. I highly recommend it to all!

JORDAN STINZIANO,
Elder, Missio Church, Syracuse, NY

The help provided in this book from Dan and Gina Trippie is not just theoretical – it has real-world practicality. I have seen this first hand in their lives, having had the pleasure of serving as their pastor, being in a couple's small group with them, and cheering for them as they entered pastoral ministry. Their story and counsel is grace-filled and gospel-centered, and is a signpost of hope for every marriage.

DR. JERRY GILLIS,
Lead Pastor, The Chapel at CrossPoint, Getzville, NY

Dan and Gina Trippie have added a necessary take to the Christian library of marriage books. While Dan and is a pastor biblically founded, this book is the practical discussion of marriage by a godly couple. Pastors, ministry leaders and Christian couples will all benefit from this. It is a frank discussion with good friends with wise direction on the most important topic for a couple.

ED MARCELLE,
Director Acts29 Northeast

Dedicated to our parents,
Dan and Diane, and Vince and Sandi,
who model an enduring marriage.

CONTENTS

WHY IS
MARRIAGE SO
DIFFICULT?

CHAPTER 1

WHY IS MARRIAGE SO DIFFICULT?

HE SAID

I remember that January morning quite vividly. The ground was crisp and the air stung like an ice pick dancing across exposed skin. As I brushed the fresh coat of snow off my truck, reality was beginning to sink in. A week in the Caribbean had dulled me to the new realities of my life. But as I sputtered off to work that morning, I can recall saying to myself, "Did I really just get married?" I realized in that moment I would never park my truck in the garage again. "Marriage is hard."

God has ordained many things to conform us into the image of his son, and among the great many sanctifiers, marriage ranks at the top! In the covenant of marriage, a man and a woman learn the intense crucible of patience, service, and above all, forgiveness. From the very beginning, God created man and woman to represent him as his vice-agents on planet earth. As image bearers, the couple was to reflect God's leadership, protection, service, and provision across the landscape of Eden. In Genesis 1:27 the author writes, "So God created man in his own image, in the image of God he created him; male and female he created them." Although God created man and woman equally in his image, he did not create them as exact replicas. Pastor and author John MacArthur, in his book *Different by Design,* states this truth as follows: "Like God, each has a rational personality. Men and women alike possess intellect, emotion, and will, by which they are able to think, feel, and choose. Humanity was not, however, created in God's image as perfectly holy and unable to sin. Nor were man and woman created in His image essentially. They have never possessed His supernatural attributes, such as omniscience, omnipotence, immutability, or omnipresence. People are only human, not at all divine."[1]

The reality that a man and a woman are not divine is something we will quickly realize once the tuxedo is returned and household chores are assigned. Understanding that individuals are designed to represent God's glory is the key to navigating the joys and the difficulties that are sure to come in marriage.

A Leader

Gina was finishing her teaching degree when we got married. In addition to working a part-time job and completing her classroom studies, she was also assigned to full-time student teaching in a home for emotionally and physically abused children. As the youngest of three and the only male child in the home, I was accustomed to a freshly made bed and a warm meal served promptly at 5:30 every evening. Much to my dismay, I entered our home on a dark February night only to find a strange new paradigm. There was nothing on the table prepared for me. If the severity of this offense was not enough, there was no smiling face waiting to serve me as I walked through the door, and ask me about my day. How could this be? I thought to myself, "This is not what marriage is about." I was not told of these things when I made the decision to trade in my bed and breakfast service for a wife. Where was my dinner?

Like many men, I had an assumption on how this marriage thing was to work. I had some church background and enough instinct to realize that men are called to be leaders in their home. Yet, just weeks into my new marriage, trouble was brewing. She didn't seem to follow very well. I began to question, "Did I marry the right woman?" . . . "Were we too young?" . . . and worse yet, "What if I married the unruly wife of Proverbs?!"

As image bearers of God, husbands are given the role of leading their wives, yet few men fully understand the nature of this leadership, and even fewer have seen it in person. Lack of understanding and scarcity of examples leave many men feeling guilty and confused as to how they are to lead in the home. In an attempt to rectify this issue, some men become timid husbands afraid to ever speak up to their wives. Others become authoritarian dictators ruling with an iron fist. Neither is an accurate model of what God intended when he placed Adam in headship over Eve. Yet, when God placed Adam in the garden, he was given several clear assignments as a representative of the Godhead.

Adam was assigned the task of imaging God by providing and protecting. In Genesis 2:16-17, God specifically told Adam that he was to work the garden and keep away from the Tree of the Knowledge of Good and Evil. Both of these assignments were given prior to Eve's creation in verse 18. The order of events becomes significant for husbands as they seek to understand the role of leadership in their marriage. First, Adam was assigned work. In Genesis 2:2, God is viewed as a being that worked in the creative process. "And on the seventh day God finished his work that he had done, and he rested on the seventh day from all his work that he had done. So God blessed the seventh day and made it holy, because on it God

DAN AND GINA TRIPPIE

rested from all his work that he had done in creation." Adam was given work in the garden so that he could mirror the glory of a God who works. As leaders in the home, men are to work not solely in a position for monetary provision, but they are to work in and around the home as well.

I don't like house work any of kind, I don't like mowing the lawn, I despise landscaping, and I don't like to clean up. I like to fish, and that's what I want to do in my free time. My early assumptions in the marriage had me believing that because I worked full-time hours 5 days a week, my nights and weekends were reserved for my comfort and serenity (and my fishing). Everything after 5:00 pm was Dan time, not to be disturbed with such matters as boiling water for pasta. Yet, the call to image God demands that men show leadership to their family through a work ethic inside and outside of the home.

A Protector

Adam was given instruction concerning spiritual protection. The command not to eat of the Tree of the Knowledge of Good and Evil was given specifically to Adam. Nowhere do we see Eve given a direct warning from God as to the perils of the tree, but rather the text assumes it was Adam's responsibility to warn his wife of sin's pitfall. This in no way exonerates Eve in her rebellion, but it does reveal why Adam's sin is charged to humanity (Romans 5:19 English Standard Version). Adam was given specific instructions to work the garden and stay away from the tree that would bring spiritual and physical death. The role of spiritual leader demands that husbands guide and protect their wives from the lure of sin.

It was not too long into our marriage that I learned my wife has a tendency to be critical. I didn't notice this while we were dating because she was perfect then. However, something happened after our honeymoon - she developed a sin nature. As leaders, husbands need to recognize first our own sin patterns then help our wives fight against theirs. Spiritual leadership means husbands help to lead spouses from the fruit that breeds death. Protecting our wives entails gently rebuking, exhorting and speaking truth in love when we notice areas of sin encroaching on her heart. I have had many people ask me to preach from 1 Corinthians 13 at their wedding, but few recognize the significance of verse 6, "Love does not rejoice at wrongdoing, but rejoices with the truth." I learned quickly, if left unchallenged, a critical spirit would not only breed bitterness in my wife's soul, but it would spread like lava to mine. Husbands, before you become self-righteous and quick to pounce here, we need to understand that Adam enjoyed the same forbidden fruit as his wife. When a man and woman are joined together as one, husbands will have a tendency to participate in the same sins as their spouse. Have you ever noticed if she is unhappy with someone or something, it will not be long before you are as well? Men, we must not give in to the weak-hearted fear so prevalent in our generation that excuses sin with the light-hearted saying, "If Momma isn't happy, then no one is happy."

To image God as a leader means that we must know our wife's sinful patterns and help lead her from that tree. The insidiousness nature of sin means that it not only kills, but it blinds its prey. It is a tragedy to see countless men sit idly by as bitterness, anger, and envy devour their wives. Many men blinded under the name of "sensitivity" coddle that which they should help to kill! Puritan Preacher John Owen once said, "Be killing sin or it will be killing you." As spiritual leaders, we are to serve our wives by helping them in the work of mortifying sin in their lives, not ignoring it or encouraging it. Spiritual leadership calls men to love their wives by doing the hard work of fighting sin alongside their spouse. Husbands are not to take up an offense for their wives but rather guide them to the one who bore our offenses on the cross.

I have been guilty of taking up an offense for Gina and failing to guide her to the cross. One day I received a call while I was at work. My young fiancée was in tears. Gina and her Maid of Honor were at the mall setting up a wedding registry at her favorite department store. Through hysterical sobbing, I was able to piece together the severity of the injustice that had taken place. Allegedly, the saleswoman at the department store informed my soon-to-be-wife that she was "not the only bride in the world," and that she would "need to be patient" while other customers were assisted. Not understanding the urgency of the situation, my princess began to educate this ill-informed woman as to the pressing nature of our wedding, which happened to be exactly 18 months away. The frantic call meant it was time to assume my role as savior. I entered the store with fire in my eyes and a determination in my heart to set the world back on its axis. As I began to confront the situation, a voice from heaven billowed throughout the store, "Security needed in the china department!" Men, providing for and protecting our wives does not mean we need to be her savior; rather, we must consistently lead her to the throne of the Savior. Marriage is a union whereby the husband and wife sanctify one another on the arduous journey towards the likeness of Christ. We ought to seek loftier goals than mere personal happiness. Our calling is to embrace the hard work of leading our marriage in the never-ending quest of holiness.

SHE SAID

Dan, my handsome new husband, helped me enter our waiting limo, carefully attempting to position the mass of tulle on my wedding dress so that he could sit beside me. Dozens of friends and family waved goodbye as we drove away from our wedding reception towards our new home. The home that we would share as husband and wife after declaring our forever love to each other. The home where we would share late-night pillow talk and cuddle up next to each other all night. The home that would be filled with our specially chosen pictures and furniture, where we would host friends for dinner, and where Fido would roam freely in our fenced-in, neatly manicured backyard. You know, all that stuff that new brides' dreams are made of. Anticipating our destination, I turned around to wave goodbye to my family, the one that I was leaving behind to start my own. It was then that my smile faded and a frightening new reality began to set in. I had a new role. I was a wife, and wives were supposed to cook, clean, and take care of other household chores. Right? The tears began to flow uncontrollably as my poor, unsuspecting husband looked at me with bewilderment. Poor guy didn't know what to do with his weeping bride! Goodness, this whole marriage thing was only easy for the first 8 hours, when the world, it seemed, revolved around me. Now what have I gotten myself into?

A Helper (my new role)

At the time of our wedding, I was a 21-year-old, madly in love girl uninformed about how to fill the role of godly wife. This ill-preparedness created much conflict in our early years of marriage. What does the Biblical role of a wife look like?

Let's read about when, why, and how the first wife, Eve, came into existence, beginning with Genesis 2:18-20, after God created Adam:

> Then the Lord God said, "It is not good that the man should be alone; I will make him a helper fit for him." Now, out of the ground the Lord God had formed every beast of the field and every bird of the heavens and brought them to the man to see what he would call them. And whatever the man called every living creature, that was its name. The man gave names to all livestock and

to the birds of the heavens and to every beast of
the field. But, for Adam, there was not found a
helper fit for him.

God created Adam and said that it wasn't good for him
to be alone and that Adam needed a helper, but God didn't
create that helper right away. First, he gave Adam the arduous
task of naming every animal on the earth. Adam thoughtfully
analyzed the characteristics of each animal before assigning
a name to them. While working through that God-given
task, Adam realized his lack of companionship. There was
no creature like him. He was a lonely man, and it was in this
loneliness that God gave Adam the one who would be his
companion, his helper, and his wife. God presented Eve to
Adam, and he responded with joyful exuberance. "This at last
is the bone of my bones and flesh of my flesh; she shall be called
Woman, because she was taken out of Man" (Genesis 2:23). At
last! Adam had his companion and helper!

During our first few months of marriage, I was a busy girl.
While completing my teaching degree, I taught during the
day, worked at night and on weekends, and finished my thesis
late at night. As for household chores, well, they mostly didn't
get done. For laundry, I had to set my alarm a couple hours
after I finally went to bed, usually around 4:00 am, to change
loads so that Dan and I would have something to wear the
next day. (Can I get a little sympathy here, please?) Anyway,
I remember one night, as I pulled the Stouffer's Lasagna out
of the microwave, that I was going to be eating alone . . .
again. I didn't know when Dan was coming home. You see,
I was the proud wife of the Assistant Chief of the Clarence
Volunteer Fire Department. Dan got called out of the home
at all hours of the day and night to either rescue a person in
distress or bravely put out a fire. When the emergency calls
were complete, Dan enjoyed hanging out at the fire hall with
the guys . . . not with his wife . . . with the guys . . . EVERY

night. Was it that he didn't enjoy my home-cooked meals or meaningful conversation while writing my paper at the same time? (I have always been a really good multi-tasker.) The truth of the matter was that Dan was a lonely man, and his only companionship was found with the guys at the fire hall. I was an emotionally and physically detached wife, which was definitely not helpful.

What does a helpful wife look like? Let's refer back to the Genesis account of Eve's creation and the biblical role of the helper. First and foremost, we must know that our true identity is an image-bearer of the Godhead (Genesis 1:26). The role of helper flows from that. There is nothing inferior or demeaning about it. God himself is our helper, and He sent the Holy Spirit to help us as well.

> "Turn to me and be gracious to me; give your strength to your servant . . . you, Lord, have helped me and comforted me." (Psalm 86:16-17)

> "The Lord is my helper; I will not fear; what can man do to me?" (Hebrews 13:6)

> "Likewise, the Spirit helps us in our weakness. For we do not know what to pray for as we ought, but the Spirit himself intercedes for us . . ." (Romans 8:26)

> "And I will ask the Father, and he will give you another Helper, to be with you forever." (John 14:16)

We, as imperfect women, will never be able to mirror our perfect God, but we must be awed by the humility of our Lord who would lower himself to help us. This certainly puts into perspective our role as our husband's helper. Wives, we are called to show compassion, to support, to defend and protect those in our care, to deliver from distress, and to comfort. We are called to be conduits of God's grace in our homes. We are called to be like Christ.[2]

I am married to a pastor. He preaches A LOT, and he is very passionate about his work. He tends to be, let's say, the talkative type. This balances my introverted, quiet nature nicely. He talks, I listen. This makes a perfect match. Or at least it would look that way on paper.

When Dan walks through the door after work, I must be prepared to give him my full attention. He likes to tell me about a new person he met, a new idea for ministry, or a new goal for the future. As I mentioned earlier, I am still a good multi-tasker, so after 18 years of marriage, I've got this routine down. As I prepare dinner, I can give one ear to Dan, the other to our sons, one eye on the stove, and the other on the recipe I am attempting to decipher. As Dan downloads his day, it occurs to me that the laundry is sitting in the dryer. I don't like to leave it there too long because then it will get wrinkled. How long has it been there? What does "gently fold in the sour cream" mean? Oh, dear, Dan absolutely cannot see me put sour cream in the dinner. He has very adverse feelings towards any white and creamy foods. How can I sneak it in now that he's home? Oh the stress of it! Is Dominick finished with his algebra homework yet? Dan's still telling me about his day, and I'm following pretty well, I think. Something about a project in the inner city, or was that at the school? I hope he doesn't ask me for feedback. He could be on to me. Perhaps I'm not the listener I thought I was.

Wives, as image bearers of God, we need to model a God who listens to our prayers, speaks encouragement to our souls, and is patient when we are restless. As your husband's companion, be present when you are together. Truly listen to him, and if that means that you need to stop talking, do so. If you are married to a man who doesn't talk a lot, don't feel the need to fill every quiet moment by talking or overwhelming him with questions. Allow your home to be a place of peace, rest, and tranquility for him.

GOD SAID

God created both man and woman in His own image. They are equally reflective of the Trinity. The three people of the Trinity are equally God, yet different in function. Genesis 1:27 says, "So God created man in his own image, in the image of God he created him; male and female he created them." Because man and woman are equal reflections of the Trinity, one is not more loved or valued than the other, but their functions are different. Marriage becomes difficult when the God-given roles or functions of the husband and wife are distorted, or when one spouse considers him or herself more significant than the other. Living in unity calls us to forms of humility that are not common to our sin-stained nature.

It can be difficult when our spouse wants to help us, correct us, or lead us, because it reminds us of our own inadequacy and pride. That's what marriage does – it makes it increasingly clear that we are dependent creatures who are made to model the interdependence of the Trinity. Although sometimes unpleasant, it is truly a great benefit to be interdependent. Your spouse sees the things you can't, or don't want, to see about yourself and watches your back for the schemes of the evil one.

YOU SAID

1) Ask your spouse how he or she perceives your work ethic, both inside and outside of the home.
2) Ask your spouse to be specific about how he or she needs your help.

3) Is there any sin in your spouse that you have been afraid to address? For example: bitterness, anger, unresolved relational conflict.

4) Ask your spouse if he or she believes that you are a good listener. Is there an area that he or she desires you to be more attentive?

5) What are the implications of your marital relationship imaging God?

HOW DO WE
COMMUNICATE?

CHAPTER 2

HOW DO WE COMMUNICATE?

HE SAID

I wanted to kill something! No seriously, I really wanted to. I began deer hunting on my fourteenth birthday but I had never shot a thing. Each year I would wake up at 4:30 am, don my warm clothes, and head out for the woods. The sun would come up and the frost would lift, but year after year I always seemed to come home empty-handed . . . until the second year of our marriage. That's when things began to change. His antlers looked like branches on a tree, and his chest resembled an NFL linebacker. This was my year! It was a dressed-out, 205 pound deer - and to think I did it the primitive way armed only with a bow and arrow.

I was beaming with pride when I drove home with my trophy hanging off the bed of my truck. A victory like this should be on display for all the world to see (or at least all who entered our new home). Gina has a real flair for decor and she likes everything to be just so. Needless to say, the deer head didn't make it into the decorating scheme she was working on. Now, I can be a shrewd manipulator, so I was sure in an hour or two I would convince her of the need for the deer head for her motif. After hours of heated deliberations, however, there was just no talking to her. So, I stopped.

Forgive

In my anger, I decided I would punish her by not talking for
almost three days (which turned out to be more painful for me
than her, because I like to talk). Sin breaks down communication
and when seeds of un-forgiveness are left unchecked, you can be
sure communication will be difficult or non-existent. Couples
may talk, but communication at the heart level requires daily
forgiveness of both major and minor offenses.

Often times, couples will say they can't communicate,
which often indicates there may be forms of resentment and
bitterness lurking below the surface. It does not matter whom
the offense is directed toward. It may be a parent, a sibling,
or the spouse, but regardless of the perpetrator, it is certain
that when unforgiveness is allowed to fester, there will be
communication difficulty. Jesus teaches us of the correlation
between communication and forgiveness in Mark 11:22-25:

> "And Jesus answered them, "Have faith in God.
> Truly, I say to you, whoever says to this mountain,
> 'Be taken up and thrown into the sea,' and does
> not doubt in his heart, but believes that what he
> says will come to pass, it will be done for him.
> Therefore I tell you, whatever you ask in prayer,
> believe that you have received it, and it will be
> yours. And whenever you stand praying, forgive,
> if you have anything against anyone, so that your
> Father also who is in heaven may forgive you your
> trespasses."

Here, and in passages such as Matthew 6:12, 14-15, Jesus
shows us that communication with God through prayer is
directly linked to the quality of forgiveness we offer to one
another. It is interesting to note that when Matthew arranges
his gospel narrative, he chooses to place Jesus' parable on
forgiveness right before his teaching on divorce (Matthew

18:15-35). Therefore, if unforgiveness breaks communication in our most intimate relationship, our relationship with God, how then will we communicate with our second most intimate relationship, the one with our spouse?

As image bearers, we must reflect the same daily forgiveness that Christ offers to his children. Colossians 3:13 commands Christians that since "the Lord has forgiven you, so you must forgive." Forgiveness is not an option that a believer can "take or leave." As reflections of God's glory on earth, married couples are made to image a God who forgives us our daily transgressions both minor and major. The question husbands and wives must constantly keep in the forefront of their mind is: "Has my spouse done something that is beyond the forgiveness of Christ?" This thinking keeps God at the center of forgiveness, thus opening the door for communication with Him first, then our spouse.

Confess

Now, I know many husbands opt out of communication with their wives claiming, "I don't have anything to say." Yeah, right! Get them in a room full of guys and they will talk for hours about work, sports, hobbies, etc. If you are one of those guys who claims you do not have anything meaningful to say to your wife, try having the courage to practice Proverbs 28:13, "Whoever conceals his transgressions will not prosper, but he who confesses and forsakes them will obtain mercy." Here is a topic starter for the dinner table: try sharing with your wife where you have sinned against her and ask her forgiveness! I imagine more than one wife might fall into her mashed potatoes to hear her husband confess that he is resentful and ungrateful for the job God has provided for him. Or, that he sinned against her by living in fear and resentment. What would it look like to have a conversation with your wife where you shared your spiritual struggles, where you have fallen short, or how you experienced victory in the last 24 hours? Husbands are far too reluctant to live out their sanctification in a way that models it for their families. In a world that does not champion repentance, ought not the spiritual leader of the home model it for his family?

Now, let me offer a few words of caution when confessing sin to your wife. Kurt Richardson, in his commentary on James, shares good insight concerning rules for confession. Although he is writing in the context of James 5:16 where confession is related to prayer and healing for congregational affairs, there is general wisdom in his words that apply further. Richardson says, "The confession of sin entails humble honesty about the fact of having committed sin, not a public retelling of the details of the act. There should not be anything sensational about the confessing our sin, nor anything that feeds sinful desire in others. Confession should entail only a humble acknowledgment of the act of sin and the joy of release from the offensiveness of those acts."[1]

When confessing sin to our spouse, we are to be honest that we have sinned, but details that would spawn temptation or a sinful response in her should be left to our private confession with Christ. My point here is not that we share our innermost lusts and temptations, but rather we model humility and repentance to our wives for the sins that have hurt them. If husbands would humble themselves to confess their sins to their wives, there would be plenty of avenues for healthy conversation - including avenues that lead to prayer.

Incarnate

When we got married, I hated shopping. Gina loves it, but the funny thing is she rarely buys a thing. She drives to the mall and walks around for hours. She scurries from store to store looking at dresses and trying on shoes, but never purchases a thing. She compares prices, takes pictures on her phone, and holds up outfits only to leave these great "deals" hanging on the rack. The whole thing makes little sense to me. I have often asked, "If you are just going to take pictures and let the items go, why can't we just go fishing instead?" However, Gina loves to shop, so after 18 years of marriage, I love to shop too.

Husbands, if communication is difficult for you, then learn to appreciate what your wife enjoys. Take an interest in her interests, show a concern for her pursuits, learn her gifts, and find ways to encourage her in them. As image bearers, we are to imitate the God who learned about us by living, dwelling, and suffering among us. The author of Hebrews says it this way: "Although he was a son, he learned obedience through what he suffered." (Hebrews 5:8) This is not to suggest that Jesus had to "learn" anything in the pedagogical sense, but rather through his suffering he experientially knows what we experience. His love for us compelled him to put on flesh and live among humanity experiencing the same laughter, sorrow, joy, and pain. Through his obedience in the incarnation, he is able to be a high priest who intimately knows us and can sympathize with us. In the same way, husbands are to love their wives just as Christ loves the church (Ephesians 5:25). It would stand to reason if Christ would love us enough to incarnate into our worlds, in like manner, husbands ought to take initiative to incarnate into their wives' interests.

My favorite movies tend to star Sylvester Stallone. Although I would contend that his movies do have romantic interests weaved into the plot, often times my wife fails to see the charm. So, in an attempt to learn what resonates with her, I have made it a practice of watching Nicholas Sparks' movies. I know I risk a lot in sharing with such transparency, but there is a reason behind such suffering. Learning the cultural art forms that resonate with our spouse helps us to learn more about them. Talk with her about why she likes certain music or authors, why she likes to connect with certain movies, and why she goes shopping and buys nothing. What I have learned is that because Gina grew up in a family that worked in the beauty industry, aesthetics hold a certain value for her. I have learned that she receives it as a profound act of love when I dress nicely for her and when I comment on her outfits. This may sound overly simplistic, but the effect that this has had on our marriage is profound. We have found many avenues of communication because I have taken an interest in things she loves. Guys, this is a win-win situation here. My wife reciprocates by showing an interest in fishing with me, while she looks hot in her cheap, fashionable clothes.

SHE SAID

I am the mother of twin teenage boys. I am a survivor. As I reflect on the years of parenting twin infants, then toddlers, then preschoolers, I can't help but marvel at the fact that we made it this far. There were days (alright, *every* day) when I needed some peace and quiet, time alone, or at the very least, time to simply empty the dishwasher or fold the laundry uninterrupted by loud noises followed by crying! Moms, you get me, right?

One night, when the boys were 3, Dan and I were serving at a church event for married couples. The boys and I met Dan at church, and then we dropped them off for childcare. Since my role at the event ended first, I was really looking forward to some quiet time in the car, followed by a few minutes to unwind before Dan brought the boys home. I was pretty confident that Dan could read my mind and know that I desperately needed that alone time. But for good measure, just before heading out, I reminded him. I know it was extremely loud and dark backstage, but I very clearly mouthed the words "I'm leaving. You will get the boys?" He nodded and we waved goodbye across the room.

About an hour later, I heard the car pull into the driveway and went to help Dan gather the boys and all their stuff. "Where are the boys?" I asked. "I thought you took them home," he responded. We left them at church - miscommunication at its finest.

Let's Talk

I know that I am not alone here. Many wives expect their husbands to read their minds, simply pick up on nonverbal cues, understand their mood swings, and give in to their unspoken desires. That is not communication, and since we were created as communicative beings, imaged after the communicative Triune God, we need to learn how to effectively communicate in a God-honoring way.

Few of us have seen healthy communication in our homes growing up. Today's media certainly does not give us healthy examples of good communication. The Bible must be our guide. God gave us the ability to speak so that we could glorify our Creator with our words. Elyse Fitzpatrick, in her book *Helper by Design,* writes, "The startling truth is that our words either serve to glorify and please Him or they exalt and please ourselves. They either portray Him properly, as a highly polished mirror reflects one who gazes into it, or they offer the world a shattered and tarnished image of His person. God has enriched our lives. Especially in our role as helpers, by granting us this gift and entreating us to employ it for His glory and our husbands' good."[2] Let's examine a few ways in which we can use our words to communicate in God-honoring ways.

Show Some Respect

We all want to be respected, especially by our spouse, the most significant human relationship we have. Our words can either show respect, honor, admiration, or disrespect, disapproval.

"Let the wife see that she respects her husband."
(Ephesians 5:33)

I have been to far too many women's gatherings (seminars, luncheons, baby showers, even Bible studies), where many wives seem to think they have a free pass to complain about their husbands under the pretext of humor, vulnerability, or advice seeking. While this type of speech is culturally acceptable, it is far from God-honoring. It is gossip and disrespect, for which there is no excuse. As one author states, if our hearts abound with disrespect, our mouths will spew disrespectful words,[3] "For out of the abundance of the heart the mouth speaks" (Matthew 12:34). Jesus modeled the speech that we are to image. He never gossiped, lied, or ridiculed. His words were full of grace, compassion, and wisdom. Wives, when speaking about our husbands publicly, or speaking with him privately, "Let your speech always be gracious . . ." (Colossians 4:6). Ask the Holy Spirit to help you resist the temptation to join in gossiping with women or criticizing your husband. The Spirit will give you strength and wisdom to communicate respectfully.

Communicate Two-Ways

You know by now that Dan tends to be the talker, and I am more of the silent type. For many couples, those generalities are reversed. Either way, how can a couple communicate without it being completely one-sided?

Ever since I can remember, I have feared public speaking. I have also become anxious when casually speaking with a small group of people. These fears and anxieties still rise up in me today. In my youth, I used the excuse that I simply wasn't gifted in the area of public speaking, but my fear is much deeper and darker than that. It is my sin nature that is the cause of much of this fear. I fear rejection. I seek the approval of man. I am afraid that vulnerability will lead to embarrassment. I find it easier and more comfortable to remain silent. However, these types of sins and insecurities break intimacy with my husband.

If you are more of the silent type, I encourage you to share your heart with your spouse. Be intentional about deep and intimate conversations. Be vulnerable. While this does not come easy for many, it will build intimacy in your marriage when you allow your spouse a glimpse of your heart. For the talkative types, I encourage you to ask meaningful questions that do not require a simple yes or no answer from your spouse. Practice the discipline of silence, and be intentional about listening.

Forgive

Almost every couple that comes to Dan and I for marital counseling confesses some degree of communication problems. Many times, when getting to the heart of the problem, the husband or wife recognizes that his or her heart is full of bitterness due to a refusal to forgive a sin his or her spouse committed against him or her.

When Dan and I got married, we were both in rebellion against God. Satisfying our fleshly desires came before our desire to honor God. Needless to say, we experienced much conflict and communicated poorly in our early years of marriage. One of my most painful memories came in our second year of marriage.

Dan was drinking too much, and it was happening on a daily basis. He was attempting to numb the pain of running from God, which was, at the very least, causing turbulence in our already fragile marriage. I was driving home from work one night when my car broke down a couple of miles from our house. You would think the easy thing to do would be to pick up the cell phone and call for help, but this was 1997, and I didn't have one! I walked to the corner convenience store to use the payphone, but it was not working. I started to panic and the store cashier allowed me to use her phone. I called our house, knowing Dan was home from work, but he didn't answer. I called again and again, knowing he was there, willing him to answer. Finally, on my seventh or eighth try, he answered. I explained where I was and that I needed him to come pick me up and take me home. He showed up a few minutes later, drunk. Thank God he didn't hurt someone on the way. I drove us both home and let my broken-down car sit illegally on the side of the road, as he was in no shape to fix it. The next morning, I reminded him we had to take care of my car right away. He had no recollection of the previous night's event.

I was scared and angry. What was happening to him . . . to us? I wanted Dan to be my rescuer, my savior, and he wasn't doing a good job. In an attempt to protect myself from more pain, I decided to close off my emotions, and in the process, I grew increasingly bitter.

Wives, we all know that there will be conflict in our marriages. Our husbands will commit offenses against us. We can choose to either forgive them or live in bitterness, resentment, and anger towards them. But how can we continuously forgive the annoyingly recurring small offenses or the seemingly more grievous ones? According to Dave Harvey, "Without understanding the depth of our sin against God and the riches of his forgiveness toward us, we will never be able to forgive others." [4]

We are self-centered beings with a sin nature that occurred after The Fall (Genesis 3). When we sin, and we all do (Romans 3:23), we must see it as high treason and offensive to a holy God. When a husband sins against his sinful wife, it pales in comparison to the grievousness of sinning against a holy, sinless, perfect God. Any sin, whether we deem it small or large, is "sufficient to warrant the full wrath of a holy God and required the blood of my Savior to take it away." [5] Jesus took away the need for punishment for our sins against God. Wives, stop punishing your husband for past and current sins against you. Freely forgive them all as Christ forgives you. Without forgiveness, there is no hope for healthy communication between you and your husband. Couples that refuse to forgive and cling to bitterness will have little that is edifying to talk about. The practice of forgiveness will pave the way to healthy communication and a God-honoring marriage.

GOD SAID

God is clear in his word that communion dies when unforgivingness flourishes. Matthew 6:15 says, but if you do not forgive others their trespasses, neither will your Father forgive your trespasses.

Confession is hard. There is nothing more painful than telling your spouse that you were wrong. Forgiveness is costly. It costs you your pride and, more importantly, it cost Jesus his life. For real communication to happen, we must model Christ who humbled himself by coming into this world to forgive our sins.

YOU SAID

1) Learn some more about your spouse's interests. Describe your perfect day to one another.
2) Talk about what specific words you both find affirming and respectful.
3) Is there anything that you need to confess to your spouse?
4) Ask your spouse if he or she feels that you are punishing him or her for any past sin.
5) Make a list of activities that both of you can do together, to image the God who incarnated into our world.

HOW CAN
WE FIND
THE TIME?

CHAPTER 3

HOW CAN WE FIND THE TIME?

HE SAID

Adulthood started somewhat old school for me. The day after my high school graduation I began to work full-time in my father's automotive business. While most of my friends were packing up for college, I was packing a lunch box heading off for work. I learned a lot of great things during this time. I learned how to work with my hands, how to interact with people more than three times my age, and how to have a love affair with money. At the age of eighteen, I was earning as much money as many adults twice my age. On the surface this sounds incredible and, of course, there were many benefits to having an early jump on life. However, some very bad habits were embedded in me in the years prior to saying, "I do."

When you are a single man, especially one who has a disposable income, you can purchase what you want when you want it. It is easy to grow accustomed to making expensive purchases on a whim without ever thinking of anyone but yourself - new golf clubs, flat screen televisions, electronic gadgets - you name it and you buy it. The selfishness produced by love of money doesn't go away once the limo pulls away from the curb of the church. Now, I realize that many men may not share my exact story, but if we are honest, how often do we think of ourselves first when it comes to money?

Money

Supporting a family is a daunting task. Unfortunately, many men fail to recognize the weightiness of providing for a wife. They continue to live as selfish adolescents holding on to toys and entertainment instead of holding their spouse. Others feel overly burdened by the charge to provide. They walk through life feeling guilt and shame for what they are not able to provide. They work long hours and never rest for fear they will not be able to give her all she deserves. Either way, the underlying root is one of selfishness and, if left unchecked, will erode away at the foundation of your marriage.

It wasn't supposed to be this way. In the beginning, Adam was given work in the garden but provision was not a burden. God had provided all the couple needed to thrive and experience joy in their relationship. It was not until after Adam gave into selfishness that work would become a burden. In Genesis 3:6, Adam stood idly by while Eve tests the forbidden fruit. "So when the woman saw that the tree was good for food, and that it was a delight to the eyes, and that the tree was to be desired to make one wise, she took of its fruit and ate, and she also gave some to her husband who was with her, and he ate." In his self-absorption, Adam sits back as if watching a lab experiment, waiting to see if his wife would really die for breaking God's commands. Once Adam believes the coast is clear, he partakes in the rebellion as well. Instead of providing spiritual protection for his wife, Adam uses her as a guinea pig to test God.

In Genesis 3:18-19, God's justice is levied on Adam's selfishness. "Thorns and thistles it shall bring forth for you; and you shall eat the plants of the field. By the sweat of your face you shall eat bread, till you return to the ground, for out of it you were taken; for you are dust, and to dust you shall return." Providing for a family would now come at the expense of the sweat of man's brow, as the earth would fight him in his attempts to support his family.

Most husbands I talk with affirm that supporting a wife brings with it some degree of anxiety and fear. Some husbands live in the fear that they will have to give up the things they hold so dear. The former high school athlete holds on to the dreams of becoming a National League All Star, so he refuses to give up any of the 5 softball leagues he is playing in. The prospect that one of their buddies might call them "henpecked" or "weak" keeps him fully invested in activities that stretch the budget, leaving no extra room for investing in his spouse. Other husbands are just plain stingy! They refuse to spend money on their wives because it will come at the expense of something they want.

Recently, I was with a couple that had approached me about performing their upcoming wedding. The young lady was sitting with eyes gazing fondly at her soon-to-be-husband. I wish I could say the same of the young man who sat next to her. As I began to ask them about their relationship, he quickly informed both of us that she would have to learn to "adjust" to the rigorous schedule and the expensive hobbies he kept. This young man raced cars on Fridays, tinkered with motorcycles on the weekends, and hung out with his buddies on weeknights. When I asked him which of these he planned to give up for the love of his new wife, he belligerently answered, "None!" The look on his fiancée's face was gut-wrenching. When I asked how he planned on supporting all his expensive hobbies while providing for his new wife, his answer was more disturbing than the first statements. Unapologetically, he announced, "I have my money and she will have her money, and that's the way it will be!" Needless to say, the couple needed to find another officiant for their wedding.

Although this story is extreme, I wish I could say this was the first time I have encountered such selfishness among husbands. Even in the church world, it is shocking to see how many men have time and money for hobbies, sports and youth lusts, while their wives sit home just longing for dinner and a movie with their husbands. I am reminded of Paul's words in 2 Timothy 2:22-23 where he says, "So flee youthful passions and pursue righteousness, faith, love, and peace, along with those who call on the Lord from a pure heart." Depending on where we place the date of 2 Timothy, many scholars suggest Timothy might have been as old as 40 when Paul pens these words to him. My point is this: men, are you so afraid to grow up that you handle your money like a pre-teen boy on his way to 7-11 with a pocket full of quarters?

While some husbands fear giving up their own selfish activities, others fear providing for the future. Fearful that a rainy day is coming that will be too large for the Lord's hand. Some men practice selfishness in other ways. Husbands can often be selfish through workaholism. Workaholism is a tricky sin because it can be wrapped in a subtle righteousness that a man is "taking care of his family." I know the insidiousness of this transgression well because I often give in to the enticing whispers of her call.

When our twins were born, they arrived two months premature. Like many premature babies, they were born with medical complications that kept them in the hospital for 2 months before we could bring them home. The weeks and months that followed kept us constantly wondering what the lasting effects would be due to their early arrival. At one point, a doctor told my wife we could expect hearing and visual disabilities and possibly an open-heart surgery. Now husbands, you would assume that with news like this a man's place would be next to his wife comforting and ministering to her, right? Well, you would be right. But that's not where I was. I went to work! Work, work, work! I hid from the support my wife needed because fears like this bounced in my head: "How can we pay these bills?" and "How will I pay for children with special needs?" as opposed to thoughts like, "How can I serve my wife?" or "What a joy my sons are alive in the world!" The reality is this: my fear drove me to a selfishness that kept me out of the house for the first 6 months of our children's lives. Although I was able to hide under the veil of "drive" and "ambition," what really lies behind the sin of workaholism is fear.

Workaholism is one of those sins that our culture champions. As Americans, we celebrate hard work and "get'er-done" mentality. However, it is often really a fear that we might be deemed as lazy that causes so many to sacrifice their marriages on the altar of work. Anxiety over what hidden expense lurks around the corner causes us to hoard and never enjoy the provision God has given. Fear that we might somehow miss out on the "American dream" causes us to break God's command to image him in Sabbath with little to no remorse. Those in professions that directly provide care for others often hide their fear under the cloak of, "I am a 'do-gooder'." In the words of Paul David Tripp, "God will not call you to break a command to fulfill another."[1]

The selfishness found in workaholism is the same selfishness found in spoiling oneself with youthful indulgences. Now, I am not saying there is anything wrong with hard work or enjoying activities and hobbies. But when these good things become ultimate things taking precedence over God and your wife, they are masking deeper sin issues concealed in the inner heart.

Contentment

Ecclesiastes 2:24-26 states: "There is nothing better for a person than that he should eat and drink and find enjoyment in his toil. This also, I saw, is from the hand of God, for apart from him who can eat or who can have enjoyment?" It is impossible to find contentment and joy in the work God has given if fear is lurking in our hearts. I have met more than one husband who trudges through his day loathing the work God has provided for him. Either his job doesn't provide enough money to enjoy all the activities of his youth or it fails to give him ironclad security for the future. Subsequently, many men live depressed vocational lives, constantly complaining to their wives about the hand they have been dealt. This constant refusal to rejoice over the work God has given us makes wives feel guilty and gives an instability wondering when and if they will have to uproot and chase down something new. Husbands, supporting a family may be a toil while we live under the curse, but even the author of Ecclesiastes recognizes we need to find enjoyment in the jobs God has provided for us.

Contentment comes only when we are taken by the glory of a God who would give generously to us. "For God so loved the world that he gave his only begotten son." Because our ultimate purpose in life is to glorify God and enjoy him forever, we will not experience joy in our work until we view it as an opportunity to reflect the glory of a God who gave himself to us. The jobs we have and the money provided from them first and foremost are an opportunity for our sanctification over and above a means to worldly achievement. Husbands, we need to understand this if we are ever to break free from the selfishness that so easily ensnares us. Once we come to the realization that our vocations are given to us from the hands of a generous God, we can be freed from selfishness by practicing generosity.

Selfishness is disarmed by applying the discipline of generosity. When husbands begin to lead their families in the truth of 2 Corinthians 9:8, "And God is able to make all grace abound to you, so that having all sufficiency in all things at all times, you may abound in every good work," they will begin to find freedom from selfishness. God has provided your family with enough resources to accomplish everything he expects you to do! If we are frustrated that we don't have enough money to live like adolescents anymore, perhaps it's because we are not expected to! If we must work ourselves beyond what is healthy for our families, we need to question if our lifestyle is commensurate with the portion God has ordained for us. Life is a vapor according to James 4:14, and the time we have to invest in our wife is short. Are we so anxious of the future that we miss the present?

If you are a man who is selfish with toys and activities, pursue freedom. What message would you send your wife if you sold your gadgets, games, and gizmos, and gave the proceeds away? What would you communicate to your bride if you sold off the things that consume your heart and used the money to win hers? Perhaps you sit her down and develop a budget that shows your treasure reveals your love, first for God then her. If you are a husband who tends to be a workaholic, what if you sat down and budgeted your time in a way that shows you are giving yourself to her? Husbands, the way we are freed from selfish desires is to be generous with our entire life.

I was scared. Gina walked in on me while I was sitting at the computer. If I could have seen my face, I am sure it was ashen like that of a zombie. I had the screen wide open and the pages laying bare on my lap. I was reading from Matthew 6:21: "For where your treasure is, there your heart will be also." I was entering purchases from my debit card into my QuickBooks software. I had never considered how much playing golf four nights a week was costing us. She was working part-time while I worked on my handicap. She never mentioned anything about my habit, but I knew we were growing apart. Our total charitable giving was less than I spent in a month on the links, and the 20 plus hours away from her was taking its toll. With a crack in my voice, I said what needed to be said, "Honey, I think we need to tithe. Including our time, too." She just smiled and said, "Whatever you think." This was the single most pivotal turning point in our marriage. We have never looked back, and to this day have never wanted to.

SHE SAID

Just a couple weeks ago, Dan and I decided to tackle the unpleasant job of cleaning the basement. Donned with rubber gloves to my elbows, safety goggles (you never know what kinds of bugs I might encounter), and a bandana to cover every strand of my hair, I was prepared. We started by opening the boxes that were still sealed from our move 5 years ago. Box after box of things that we haven't needed or missed in 5 years. Are we some kind of hoarders? As I was loading the items into a bin labeled "donate," Dan shouted with glee, "Look what I found!"

It was a dusty, yellowed photo album that I had no recollection of. Dan walked towards me smiling at the first page of photos. I took one look and the sweet memories came flooding back . . . Summer 1989. Our first official date.

Life is moving too fast. Those photos – they seem like they were taken ages ago. Our innocent laughter is reflective of a season of life when work pressures, family obligations, or friends' expectations didn't weigh us down. Wives, in this busy and stressful season of life, how can we find time to enjoy life with our husbands again?

Priorities

In order to find time to enjoy your husband, you must first enjoy Jesus. You can't enjoy Jesus without spending time in His Word and in prayer. This is a discipline that must occur on a daily basis. Write it into your schedule before anything else. Wives, believe me, I am preaching to myself here. Quite often, looking at my calendar gives me heart palpitations, and

I cannot fathom how I can make it through the week without more coffee, less sleep, and dropped balls. That anxiety that I feel serves as an indicator of misplaced zeal. Wives, we manage to find time for things that we are zealous for, don't we? We can squeeze in a few minutes for Facebook or Pinterest, can't we? How about for lunch with girlfriends, cleaning the house, or reading to the kids? Have you used time for taking a much-needed nap, working out, or volunteering at the school? None of these are wrong . . . unless they come before your time with Jesus.

So many wives tend to be multi-taskers, trying to juggle every ball while attempting to please our children, husband, and friends at the same time. God's desire is that we put our relationship with Him before any other relationships or tasks. He has sought that with us from the beginning (Genesis 1:26). He continued pursuit of an intimate relationship with us by sending his Son to pay the price for our sin. Because of Jesus' work on the cross, he made a way for you and I to have an intimate relationship with him, a holy God.

God longs for intimacy with you. He pursues a relationship with you, wanting you to respond to his love and desire for time with you. He wants you to know him to the fullest. This amazing opportunity for a relationship with the Creator and Savior must be first priority. His command is to love him with all your heart, all your soul, and all your might (Deuteronomy 6:5). God comes before your husband, before your children, and before your friends. If your relationship priorities are misplaced, you are falling into idolatry (Exodus 20:3) and setting up your marriage for disappointment and failure. No human relationship can give you what only God can.

Jesus modeled this intimacy with God for us. He knew what it was like to lead a busy life, more busy than you or I could imagine. In Mark 1, we read that Jesus' days were filled with traveling from town to town preaching the gospel, healing the sick, teaching in the synagogue, and casting out demons.

As His fame spread, crowds of people would gather around Him just to be in His presence, learn from His teaching, and be made healthy. Even with the whole city gathering at His door (Mark 1:33), Jesus made intimacy with God His priority. While His disciples were still sleeping, Jesus went to a secret place to commune with God. "And rising very early in the morning, while it was still dark, he departed and went out to a desolate place, and there he prayed" (Mark 1:35). As Matthew Henry states: "His retirement to his private devotion set us an example of secret prayer. Though as God he was prayed to, as man he prayed. Though he was glorifying God, and doing good in his public work, yet he found time to be alone with his Father; and thus it became him to fulfill all righteousness." [2]

Wives, God longs to commune with you (Isaiah 30:18), and his grace will give you the desire and discipline to spend time with Him as He continues to conform you more and more in His image (Romans 8:29). Pray for the discipline of time in your life. Pray for the Spirit's help in overcoming the temptation of putting other people, activities, or sleep before Jesus. Ask God for the wisdom and courage to say "no" to anything that comes before Him so that you can devote time every day to commune with Jesus. Then, and only then, will you be able to truly enjoy your husband and your marriage the way God intended.

Work

A few years ago, I snagged my dream job. I am a bridal consultant. Ever since I was a little girl, I have had a fondness for the white dress and all that it signifies: beauty, purity, forever love, happiness, security. Now, I have the privilege of helping brides find their dress. The dress of all dresses. The one that they will wear to walk down the aisle to pledge their love and commitment to their groom. The dress that makes every head turn, every jaw drop, and every lover's eyes tear up.

The one that will be remembered for decades to come through photos in the scrapbook and on the bedroom wall. It's the most important dress they will ever wear, and when they put the dress on for the first time and realize that it is the one, I have the joy of celebrating the moment with them, shedding a few tears, clapping with excitement, and giving congratulations. I love my job!

It is not a full-time job, nor a high paying one. Recently, however, I received a job offer that would pay three times as much as I earn now . . . three times! Oh, the breathing room that this income could afford us! My family rejoiced in this apparent blessing from God, while praying over how to leave my current job well. As we were beginning to make plans to move forward with this transition, Dan and I started to consider the implications. First, the added hours of my new job would make it difficult to maintain weekly attendance at our corporate church gathering on Sundays. Second, the scheduled work hours would interfere greatly with time with my husband and children. Third, what message would I be sending to my children and my co-workers by leaving a job that I loved solely for the purpose of making more money?

Let's consider the godly woman described in Proverbs 31:10-31. She is truly remarkable because she does everything well. Here are some of her attributes:

- Godly character
- Trustworthy
- Hardworking
- Wise
- Generous
- Gracious
- Contributes to her family's financial needs
- Manager
- Investor
- Manufacturer of goods

- Charitable
- Teacher
- Promotes her husband

I'm thinking that this woman is a bit too remarkable . . . don't you? If you and I compare ourselves to her, we probably fall short, but this passage was not written to make us feel inadequate or guilty. Missing from the passage are her limitations, failures, struggles, and sins (surely she has all of these). Only her successes and godly attributes are described. For this reason, she is a picture of an ideal wife – one that can never be fully reached by us humans with a sin nature. However, it does give us an example for every Christian (man and woman) to imitate, because the Proverbs 31 woman is an imitator of Christ.

When considering a job offer or taking on any task, activity, or relationship, for that matter, we should consider the implications of this text in Proverbs. I believe an important principle underlying this passage is that the efforts of the wife, in every instance, should contribute to the well-being of the family. Any employment the wife might have which is detrimental to the spiritual and moral well-being of the family, in my estimation, would be wrong. This principle applies as much to the husband as it does to the wife.[3]

The new job offer that I received, Dan and I decided together, would not contribute to the well-being of our family. I have to be honest with you. There was a lump in my throat when I declined it. I was saying goodbye to monetary provision that could afford us a new car, opportunities for travel, and the ability to put our boys through college. However, I would also have to say goodbye to making breakfast for my sons and sending them off to school every day, enjoying weekly fellowship and teaching of God's Word at church, and "couch time" with my husband on certain weeknights. Those are opportunities that I could not miss. That is precious time that I could not give up.

Wives, time is the one thing that we cannot get more of. We can't multiply it and we can't get it back. We need to be ruthless about protecting and maximizing the short time that we do have with our husbands. And we can rest. Rest in the freedom of knowing that God will provide for all of our needs (Philippians 4:19) as we image Him in our marriages.

GOD SAID

God promises to provide for all of our needs. Genesis 1:29-31 tells us, "And God said, 'Behold, I have given you every plant yielding seed that is on the face of all the earth, and every tree with seed in its fruit. You shall have them for food. And to every beast of the earth and to every bird of the heavens and to everything that creeps on the earth, everything that has the breath of life, I have given every green plant for food.' And it was so." It is an ongoing battle to trust God for provision. Yet, from the beginning, God saw to it that man and woman would have everything they need for survival. The antithesis of faith is fear. Fear is what drives us to become workaholics, ungrateful, and idolatrous.

God has given you all that you need for a healthy rhythm of life. You already have enough time to accomplish all that He has for you. Use it wisely.

YOU SAID

1) Ask your spouse to list your relationships in order of priority, based on his or her observation of your life.
2) Ask how your spouse feels about the way you spend your leisure time.

3) Ask your spouse to describe what it looks like for him or her to feel appreciated by you.
4) Discuss how much time together each week would make a significant investment in your marriage.
5) As a couple, develop a budget for your time and money that includes the priorities of God, marriage, and future.

WHY ISN'T
OUR SEX LIFE
AS GOOD AS
I EXPECTED?

CHAPTER 4

WHY ISN'T OUR SEX LIFE AS GOOD AS WE EXPECTED?

HE SAID

I wrote letters (fifteen of them to be exact) scratched out in handwriting resembling an 8-year-old's and stuffed them in utility bill envelopes. Nevertheless, I wrote fifteen letters recounting one high-point memory from each of the first fifteen years of our marriage. Every day for the two weeks following our anniversary, I made sure Gina had a note recounting how much I love her and how my attraction to her has grown stronger over the years. Each night, while she was preparing herself for bed, I would sneak a note under her pillow like a mischievous tooth fairy anxiously awaiting her reaction to this sneaky act. I am a romantic. If you are not, trust me, it's worth your while to become one!

Sex is perhaps one of the most exhilarating and frustrating activities of marriage. When sex in marriage is good, men will find a deep sense of confidence and courage to lead your family well. When sex is difficult, men will fight against insecurity, fear, and anger. Unfortunately, many of our expectations for sex are shaped by an overly exaggerated culture. A recent study done by the Kaiser Family Foundation reports the average young person ingests over 53 hours a week of media in some fashion.[1] Whether it be television, internet, or movies, all these media paint an unrealistic portrait of sex. If you are a man who was exposed to pornography at an early age, these expectations will only become more distorted. Our sex-crazed culture has exaggerated sex to the point where men often enter marriage programmed with irrational fantasies that neither he nor his wife can possibly achieve.

In pre-marriage counseling, I will often ask both the man and the woman to give me their thoughts on sex. I will ask questions like: "What were you told growing up?" "What assumptions did your religion leave you?" "What did your parents teach you (either implicitly or explicitly) about sex?" A generation ago, I might have expected largely negative responses as couples shared what they learned about sex. Answers such as, "My youth pastor told me never to do it before marriage"; or my priest said, "Fight temptation!"; or my parents said, "You don't want to get pregnant, do you?!"

Today, responses like these are few and far between. Two hundred years of cultural teaching unpinned by a belief that every human has the right to pursue personal pleasure has eroded any thought of restraint. When I ask men in premarital counseling to share their thoughts on sex, seldom do I hear anything about restraint until marriage. Furthermore, rarely do I hear men give a compelling vision for sex at all. When asked to share a vision and purpose for the act of sex, few (if any) can think beyond immediate physical gratification and procreation. Don't get me wrong, sex is fun and it does make babies! However, a vision for sex that is confined to only personal pleasure and procreation is not a big enough vision to fight the unreal expectations society has painted. If a man's vision for sex is limited to personal pleasure, it will not be long before he is either disappointed and angry or emasculated and ashamed. Men need a vision for sex that views it as an act of worship, as opposed to an idol to be worshiped.

Theology of Sex

A right vision for sex again begins with a right understanding of the creation account. Again, we turn to Genesis 1:26-28 where we see God creating man and woman in his image. In verse 26, we see God referring to himself in the plural form, "Let *us* make man in our image . . ." This is very important to understand as it relates to our vision for sex. After the Trinity creates humans, the Godhead commands them to reflect his image on the earth by sending them out to fill the planet. God gives them the command to have sex, *"Be fruitful and multiply,"* so the earth will be filled with more image bearers. Yes, men, it is a command of God to have sex with our wives! (It is good to follow the commands of God!) However, more than procreation is in view here. One chapter later, God tells man to leave his father and mother and become one flesh with his wife.

God creates man and woman for the purpose of reflecting his image on earth. Genesis 1:26 reveals that his image is plural while at the same time bonded in oneness. God the Father, God the Son, and God the Spirit all exist as unique individuals while at the same time existing as one unified Godhead who are all equally divined. The Trinity is made up of distinct individuals while at the same time bonded in unique oneness. When a man and woman become one flesh, the two become a living word picture of the God who is uniquely one while at the same time distinctly individual. Sexual intercourse thus becomes a way to reflect the glory of the Trinity. Individuals become uniquely one while at the same time remain distinct individuals. Why is sex addressed in the opening chapters of redemptive history? Because it is rooted deep in the purpose of humanity itself.

Furthermore, the act of sex is viewed between a man and woman in the context of a covenant relationship. Genesis 2:24 uses the term *"leave"* as an indication of monogamous covenant relationship. Kenneth A. Matthews states in his commentary on Genesis: Marriage is depicted as a covenant relationship shared by man and woman. Monogamy is clearly intended. "Leave" and "cling" are terms commonly used in the context of covenant, indicating covenant breach (e.g., Deut 28:20; Hos 4:10) or infidelity.[2] By the end of Genesis 1 and 2, we see God giving to humans a vision for sex that is greater than pleasure and procreation. By the end of the first two chapters of redemptive history, we see that when a male husband and a female wife become one flesh, it is an act of worship and magnification of God's Trinitarian glory. How is that for a higher vision of sex!

Learn to Get it Right!

Having a biblical vision for sex frees men from being overly consumed by it or feeling insecure because of it. When we have a view from a biblical and theological perspective, it allows men to move past the multitude of images inundating us, which allows us to pursue sex in a selfless and healthy way seeking to honor God. Philippians 2:3 says, *"Do nothing from rivalry or conceit, but in humility count others more significant than yourselves."* Men, sex with your wife is not about you and your physical desires first and foremost. When we view sex as an act of worship pleasing to God, then we find that satisfying our wife takes priority over pleasing ourselves. Sex becomes a real and tangible act of serving our spouse in a way that considers her desires more significant than yours.

Men, the reality is that it takes time to learn how to please your wife sexually. As much as you may think you have this all down, you would do well to leave those opinions to your wife's discretion! Men, lose your pride! Ask your wife how you are doing at meeting her physical desires in bed. I know this might be an awkward conversation, so don't bring it up over nachos and queso dip or while she is folding laundry after a long day of chasing kids around. Timing is everything, so plan a time and place that is appropriate to have a serious discussion about sex. Don't try to mask the awkwardness with humor or another form of deflection. Be serious, show her it is important to you that you know and understand her wishes and desires.

Be a Student

A woman's body is not wired like a man's. Fifteen thousand nerve fibers reside in the female pelvic area, which nearly doubles that of the male anatomy. These nerve fibers are connected to more than eight thousand nerve endings, many of which are internal. My point here is the female body is complicated and it requires a husband to do some homework on the female anatomy. Television and movies portray sexual intercourse as an effortless act that brings both parties into a rapturous world of pleasure and ecstasy simply from touching each other. Unfortunately, many young couples enter marriage expecting this to be the case. Disappointment, frustration, and even shame occur when the realities of anatomical differences become known. A large reason why so many women struggle to achieve orgasm during sexual intercourse is because men have not learned how the female body is physically designed.

This might sound like a tenth grade health class issue, but the truth is most of us were too immature to understand the information that was being taught. We were too young physically and certainly too immature spiritually to know why knowledge of anatomy is so vital for marriage. God has designed specific parts of your wife's body for the sole purpose of giving her pleasure, and it is your responsibility to figure out how to make that happen. There is a wealth of information available to you where you can learn how your wife's sexual organs work. Husbands, do not assume you have it all figured out. Be a student, but a cautious one. Let your wife find teaching resources on sex and the female anatomy and relay the information to you. There are good Christian resources available but I would still suggest having your wife read and approve any material relating to the functioning of her body. We are visual beings, and many of the resources online or in bookstores will only open the door to temptation. If you are a man who has viewed pornography, the gospel forgives and heals you, but you are still left with scars from your past. Asking your wife to help you "learn" her body will not only protect you from temptation but also allow her to fulfill her God-ordained design to be your helper. As you lean on your wife as she shares how her body works, the gospel's power of restoration can be celebrated at deeper levels. Genesis 2:25 says Adam and Eve were naked and not ashamed. Perhaps one of the most intimate and vulnerable experiences married couples can have is sharing with one another about their bodies. As authentic conversations arise, husbands and wives can experience the purity and joy of learning how to serve each other sexually as God intended.

It Takes Time

I have always hated the cliché, "Women are crock pots, and men are microwaves." I understand the premise, but the analogy seems silly to me. I think a more fitting analogy would be something like, "Women are like barbecue, the longer they smoke, the more tender they become." It goes without saying that it takes longer for a woman to prepare for sex than a man. Not only does her body physiologically require more time to prepare, but also a woman's emotional preparation takes longer as well. Dr. Kevin Leman, in his book *Sex Begins in the Kitchen*, describes how women emotionally prepare for sex as they interact with their husband throughout the entire day.[3]

Women need romance before they are ready to engage sexually with their husbands, and romance takes time.

Romance is not something that happens fast. Romance takes thought, planning, preparation, and perseverance. What men often think is romantic is a far cry from what a women finds idyllic. Just as a husband must study his wife's body to know what she desires, he must also study her psychology to discover what she finds romantic. Men, don't get tripped up on the idea of being romantic. Once you know what your wife desires, you will realize how simple it can be to practice romance throughout the day.

My wife likes coffee prepared with one cream and one Splenda packet (not Equal and not sugar - only Splenda). Every morning, I make sure she has a fresh cup of coffee ready and waiting for her to begin her day. This might not seem like much but I have learned this is one of the most romantic things I can do for her. Taking a little time to prepare coffee in the morning helps the process of ending the day in a good way! Husbands, figure out how to romance your wife not only in big ways but also in small subtle acts that show her that you are thinking more about her than yourself.

Recently, I was informed of an app for the iPhone called, "Book on Her." This app allows a husband to record a multitude of important information about his wife such as her dress size, ideas for surprise gifts, her favorite romantic restaurants, or quirky things that might make her laugh. Books such as C.J. Mahaney's *Sex, Romance, and the Glory of God* can help spur you on to think more romantically. The idea to remember here is that it takes effort and time to learn how to romance your wife. However, once you learn how, you will find it easier to make romance a part of your daily routine. Too many men stop romancing their wives once vows are exchanged and diapers begin to be changed. I would contend that real romance does not happen until several years of married life together.

As this book is being written, Gina and I are approaching 19 years of marriage. If there is one thing we have discovered about a healthy sex life, it is that it takes years to nurture. In our experience, it took at least a decade before we had grown in romance, intimacy, and the spiritual maturity to experience the fullness of God's gift in sex. Sadly, too many couples call it quits before they ever experience the joy of healthy sexual union together. If you have not yet experienced a fulfilling sex life in your marriage, I would draw your attention to Paul's words from 1 Corinthians 13:4: "Love is patient." Humans are intricate beings, and it takes years of growth and humility before we can fully share the depth of oneness brought on in the marriage bed. If your spouse and you are not where you desire to be sexually, be encouraged that as you grow in your knowledge of Christ and knowledge of each other, your sexual relationship will grow more fulfilling. I tell all couples who come to me for pre-martial counseling: "It is going to take ten years of practice before you figure sex out. So, practice often!"

SHE SAID

Be honest. Did you skip right to this chapter? I probably would, with the intention of going back to read through from the beginning, of course! Here's what you need to know before continuing through this chapter: I am not interested in writing about sex for shock value or with scandalous illustrations. My prayer is that this section, written for wives, is helpful and gives hope for growing in sexual intimacy with their husbands. God, in His amazing grace, gave us the gift of sex for many good reasons including pleasure (Song of Solomon 2:8-17; 4:1-16), making babies (Genesis 1:28), oneness (Genesis 2:24), and for protection (1 Corinthians 7:2-5). Sex, in the context by which God created it, is a really, really, really good thing. So, why then are many couples' sex lives rarely as good as they had expected them to be?

Protection

I'm referring to protection from sin, of course. What were you thinking I meant? Let's start by taking another look at the purpose for which God created women. Wives, remember that God designed us to be our husband's helper (Genesis 2:18). As you seek to fulfill that role in his life, remember that includes helping him to resist sin.

> But because of the temptation to sexual immorality, each man should have his own wife and each woman her own husband.
> (1 Corinthians 7:2)

For the Christian, a healthy and pleasurable marital sex life is a safeguard against temptation. It releases normal sexual tension, which, in turn, guards against sexually immoral temptations. In our culture of instant gratification, self-fulfillment, media-fueled pornography, and a fear of calling sin what it is, we as wives must fight for the moral protection of our husbands. Moral protection is not just a pleasant byproduct of marital intimacy. It is the core reason for marital intimacy.[4]

Visual Stimulation

Wives, there are many practical ways in which you can help protect your husband from sexual immorality. Knowing that men tend to be visual, I personally enjoy making sure that Dan's eyes have no reason to wander, and that he is captivated by ways in which I have visually delighted him. And there is no better place to learn how to do this than from scripture. Yes, we can learn how to stimulate our husbands from the Bible . . . what a book! Let's read about how the wife meets her husband's need for visual stimulation in Song of Solomon 4:1-6:

Behold, you are beautiful, my love,
   behold, you are beautiful!
Your eyes are doves
   behind your veil.
Your hair is like a flock of goats
   leaping down the slopes of Gilead.
Your teeth are like a flock of shorn ewes
   that have come up from the washing,
 all of which bear twins,
   and not one among them has lost its young.
 Your lips are like a scarlet thread,
   and your mouth is lovely.
Your cheeks are like halves of a pomegranate
   behind your veil.
Your neck is like the tower of David,
   built in rows of stone;
 on it hang a thousand shields,
   all of them shields of warriors.
Your two breasts are like two fawns,
   twins of a gazelle,
   that graze among the lilies.
Until the day breathes
   and the shadows flee,
I will go away to the mountain of myrrh
   and the hill of frankincense.

There are many occasions where the husband praises his wife for appealing to his need for visual stimulation (1:8-10, 15, 6:4-10, 7:1-9). I love her response to his praise in 7:10: "I am my beloved's, and his desire is for me."

How sweet it is for a wife to know that she is solely her husband's, and that his desire is only for her. She strives to please him visually, and he praises her for it, giving her confidence in his faithfulness. We can take some cues from her.

Here are some more practical ideas to try in order to visually stimulate your husband:

- Take time every day to shower, shave, style your hair, apply makeup
- Dress in clothes that flatter your figure
- Keep your figure as fit as possible
- Flash him
- Dress in front of him
- Dance for him
- Wear sexy lingerie to bed
- Sleep naked
- Hang a mirror near your bed
- Don't stop here - ask your husband what he would add to this list

You may be thinking that this is an uncomfortable challenge because you hate your body. I'm not overly confident about mine either, ladies. Those twins did quite a number on my abs, I have a roadmap of stretch marks on my stomach, and I am realizing that there is a relationship between gravity and aging that is not beneficial to a woman's figure. It's not just ageing and babies that cause a woman to doubt her beauty. The young wife in Song of Solomon 1:6 begs her betrothed not to gaze at her because she was ashamed of her dark tan from working in the fields (apparently spray tanning is not a thing of the past). Wives, as you and your husband move towards sexual intimacy and oneness, his desire for you will grow and his eyes will see that which is beautiful to him.

Wives, remember, you were bought with a price (1 Corinthians 6:18-20). While you may not see a picture of physical perfection when you look in the mirror, remember, you were created to image a perfect, loving, and fearless God. Have confidence (1 John 4:16-18).

Physical Intimacy

In Song of Solomon, we see a beautiful picture of ideal physical intimacy. The one-flesh relationship (Genesis 2:24) is the most intense physical intimacy and the deepest spiritual unity possible between a husband and wife. Marriage is to be modeled on the unified, mutually submissive, intimate relationship between Christ and His bride, the church. We are to model Christ's love to serve and to give to our husbands, as Christ does for us (Mark 10:45).

> The husband should give to his wife her conjugal rights, and likewise the wife to her husband. For the wife does not have authority over her own body, but the husband does. Likewise, the husband does not have authority over his own body, but the wife does. (1 Corinthians 7:3,4)

By serving your husband sexually, you are protecting him from temptation, as well as giving him his conjugal rights. Yes, that's correct: HIS rights to YOUR body. Hang on there! If you are thinking about throwing this book at the wall, stay with me for a moment (actually, for the rest of the book, please). In this scripture, notice that Paul is referring to mutual submission for the good of the other. You have rights that your husband must meet too. His body is yours; you are one (Genesis 2:24).

Since Dan has already addressed the husband's responsibility in serving the needs of the wife, the purpose of writing this section will be for addressing the responsibility of the wife.

Notice that Paul first addresses the husband. It is his responsibility to fulfill his wife's conjugal rights. Wives, we have needs too, and our husbands need to learn how to get it right. However, the only way he can learn is if you clearly communicate what does and does not work, and allow him repeated opportunities to practice. Wives, if you do not communicate or allow him to practice different techniques, he will become embarrassed and rejected. You, on the other hand, will become increasingly frustrated. Help him succeed in fulfilling you sexually.

> Do not deprive one another, except perhaps by agreement for a limited time, that you may devote yourselves to prayer; but then come together again, so that Satan may not tempt you because of your lack of self-control. (1 Corinthians 7:5)

Scripture is clear that married couples should have frequent sex, with only one exception: if the couple mutually agrees to temporarily abstain for an extenuating circumstance requiring a time of intense prayer. Other than that, have sex, and have it often. Obedience to this is holy and pleasing to God. Although most women recognize that they probably don't have as much sex as they should (or wish they could), they rarely think about this abstinence as sin. Yet, when we refuse our husband's attentions, we're actually robbing (depriving) him of what is rightfully his, while exposing him to unnecessary temptation.[5] As your husband's helper, one way that you can help him pursue holiness and resist temptation is to fulfill him sexually.

Danger

> Catch the foxes for us,
>   The little foxes
> That spoil the vineyards,
>   For our vineyards are in blossom.
> (Song of Solomon 2:15)

A satisfying, frequent sexual relationship is not something that just happens when the minister pronounces you husband

and wife. It needs to be built over time by years of mutual effort and reliance on the grace of God. Failure to cultivate this is a danger to your marriage. In Song of Solomon 2:15, "foxes" are those dangers that can destroy your sexual union and your marriage. Whatever we find a hindrance to us in that which is good we must put away. Spouses are commanded to "catch" them before the marriage fails. Here are some problems, or foxes, that are a danger to your sexual union and to your marriage:

Exhaustion

This is probably the most common reason that I hear from wives for lack of frequent sex in their marriages. It's that overscheduled day and undisciplined use of time that can kill your sex life. Remember, you will find time to do the things that you are zealous for. Pray for the zealous desire and energy to serve your husband sexually. Is there a time of day that you find you have more energy? If you have young children, can you put them to bed earlier every night to give you and your husband alone time? If you have teenagers like us, can you put yourselves to bed earlier? How about that lunch hour? I know of a really good way to get your husband to come home for lunch . . .

Lack of Enjoyment

If a couple does not enjoy sex, it is unlikely that they will engage in it frequently. Wives, if your husband is unskilled at giving you sexual pleasure, gently and patiently communicate your desires, and allow him opportunities to practice. If you are simply bored with your monotonous sex life, what is it going to take to get out of that rut? A trip to Victoria's Secret (or the resurrection of your honeymoon lingerie) and a bottle of massage oil can go a long way. Need some fresh ideas to spice things up? There are plenty of non-pornographic, Christian resources available for you to look into.

Sin

Many women struggle with frequent sex because their perspective of it has been damaged by past sin. Guilt over sexual sins can inhibit your ability to enjoy sex with your husband. Wives, there is freedom from the guilt, and forgiveness available to you through Jesus Christ. If we confess our sins, he is faithful and just to forgive us our sins and to cleanse us from all unrighteousness (1 John 1:9). If you continue living in guilt and shame, you are not trusting God. Confess and repent, and then don't ever bring it up to God again, because He has forgotten it (Hebrews 10:17). He no longer holds you accountable for forgiven sin.

If a sin has been committed against you such as abuse, abandonment, or unfaithfulness, know that it was never God's intent for you to be hurt. He is pained and angered by the injustice committed against you more than you know. Cling to Him for comfort, strength, and healing. Do not be ashamed and do not dismay. He is with you. He will help you and uphold you with his righteous right hand (Isaiah 41:10). If your marriage is struggling because of the harmful effects of sin, we encourage you to seek biblical counseling from a professional biblical counselor or pastor. In addition to that, a good resource for women struggling in this area is *Intimate Issues*, by Linda Dillow and Lorraine Pintus.

You Can Do It!

There are many other reasons wives struggle with sex - from hormones to headaches and from different sex drives to different bed times. These struggles must be addressed in order to protect your marriage. While oneness between husband and wife is certainly more than having a sexual relationship, it is not less than that. It needs to be cultivated with effort, communication, grace, and a servant's heart. Meditate on the scripture – God's Word will show you how to love and serve your husband, cultivating a sexual unity that can only build and protect your marriage.

GOD SAID

Why isn't sex as good as you expected it to be? Who or what defines "good" sex for you? Your definition should not come from the media, your friends, the authors of marriage books, or counselors. Only you and your spouse can define what good sex is in your marriage, and this is based on intimate conversation rooted in scripture and for the glory of God.

God's plan for sex is very, very good. He has given us the gift for our pleasure, for procreation, and for His glory. The sexual, one-flesh union is representative of the union of the Trinitarian God (Genesis 2:24). Any time a husband and wife become one flesh, they are glorifying the God that created them.

Sex is also complicated. No other act seems to be rooted so deeply into our personhood. Our culture trivializes sex making it the punch line of every joke or by making it the pinnacle of life's existence. Sex is neither something to be taken lightly nor something that ultimately gives a person value. Sex between a husband and wife, when done to the glory of God, is an act of worship which portrays the oneness of God. God takes sex seriously because it deals with the lives of those who bear His image.

Regardless of how you viewed or experienced sex in the past, if it is done God's way, your sex life can be much better than you ever expected.

"Eat, friends, drink, and be drunk with love!"
(Song of Solomon 5:1)

YOU SAID

1) Are you satisfied with the frequency of sex in your marriage?
2) What are some of the "foxes" or dangers to your sexual union? Talk about how you can overcome this together.
3) Are you making an effort to learn more about your spouse? Talk about what you need to study up on to improve your sex life.
4) What do you define as a good sex life?

HOW CAN OUR MARRIAGE SURVIVE PARENTING?

CHAPTER 5

HOW CAN OUR MARRIAGE SURVIVE PARENTING?

HE SAID

After 3 rings on the shop loud speaker, I was immediately called into the office. I was working in my father's auto shop in the days before cell phones when the call came. Something inside told me all was not well. We had tried for months to get pregnant and everything seemed to be going alright so far. Just weeks earlier we had heard our child's heartbeat, but as we all know, the first trimester can be an unstable time. "Dan!" she said, "I am going to the doctor. Something is wrong!" My heart pounded in my chest. "What if . . .", "How will I . . .", "She's going to be devastated." Gina quickly informed me that her mother was already there, and I would not have time to get home. "Mom will take me, and I will let you know as soon as I can." She hung up the phone without giving me the location where to meet them.

It was an hour and a half later when she walked in the door looking quite pale. My heart sunk knowing there would be no words to comfort her. She moved in close extending her hand without a word. Her smile was overwhelming as she handed me the foggy black and white photo. The picture looked like an over-exposed snapshot from one of those shopping mall photo machines. "What is this?" I naively replied. Gina gently smiled and said, "Our babies."

The day I found out we were having twins will forever be etched in my mind. So many emotions flooded my head I could hardly sort them all out. I must admit many of the thoughts that day were not about the joy of fatherhood but rather the fear of it. "How will I provide?" "I'm so impatient; I will lose my temper." "What if I fail?" Fatherhood calls a man to walk the tightrope of great responsibility while, at the same time, trusting in God's inexhaustible grace. The reality is, however, many men tend to live out their roles as fathers with a gnawing sense of fear and anxiety.

Role

The weight of being a father resides in men because we are created to be image bearers. Throughout the scriptures, God has revealed himself as a Heavenly Father who protects, provides, corrects, cares for, and loves his children. Although there is no revelation of God as Father in the Old Testament equivalent to that of Jesus in his prayer to *Our Father*, the character of his fatherhood is implicitly spread across the totality of scripture. In the first five books of the Bible, we see God as a father who gives life and guides his children. In the poetic books, God is revealed as a provider of rain (Job 38:28), protector of the innocent (Psalm 68:5), and a father of compassion. The prophetic books also reveal that God is a father who loves his children enough to discipline them while, at the same time, providing the way of restoration (Jeremiah 25:8-14). By the time Jesus utters the words "Our Father" in The Lord's Prayer, the concept of a loving God had been lost by many of the Jews of that day. The 1st century Roman culture was one of multiple gods, all of whom were thought to be distant, captious, and fearsome. So, when Jesus reintroduces the concept of God as a Heavenly Father, he is recapturing the essence of intimacy with God. The revelation of God as Father was in stunning contrast to the pagan gods of the day.[1]

Comparable to the first century, today's world has lost the concept of God as Father. Few people today have a healthy view of God as a loving and just father because they have never seen or experienced a loving and just earthly father. Today's culture is imploding at unprecedented rates largely due to the breakdown in the role of father. Industrialization has kept fathers separated from families by forcing these men to work long hours away from home. The women's liberation movement has left many men uncertain as to their value in the home. In addition, the rampant rate of divorce has resulted in an entire generation without any visible models of a man functioning daily in the home. Comparatively, same-sex marriage is sadly perverting the concept of biblical masculinity altogether. The effects of the last 100 years of cultural shifts have left men confused and scared when it comes to fatherhood. Men know they are expected to be good dads, yet having a model to emulate is as foreign as moon dust from the planet Alderraan.

Quite simply, fatherhood requires men to model God. Perhaps the single most important element men must realize when parenting children is that you are a visual representation of God to your child. The way your children experience you as a father will have a significant impact on the way they will view God. Men, you are an image bearer! Dads, the single most important thing we must know about parenting is that every day we are forming our child's view of God.

Unity

Since fathers represent God to their children, every father must remember that God is a God of unity. We have already seen how the trinity affects sex between a husband and wife, but the trinity also has implications for how we parent our children. A key role a father plays in the home is to create a sense of unity among all family members. All too often, men bring discord and disunity into their families without ever realizing the damage they are causing. In Genesis 25:28-34, we see firsthand what happens when a father allows disunity in the home. Isaac loved his son Esau more than he loved his son Jacob. The effects of the discord he sowed brought tension to Isaac's marriage and sent shockwaves throughout history. Later on we see the damage caused as Jacob sows seeds of disunity in his family by favoring Joseph more than his other children. Admittedly, God providentially used these families to fulfill his redemptive plan, but the result came through years of pain and family turmoil.

Although most fathers never intend to cause division in their families, it happens often as careless words slip out unnoticed. Words like, "Why can't you get grades like your sister?" or "Your brother did well in sports; why do you struggle so much?" or "This is my difficult child." Subtle or unsubtle words of favoritism can cause devastating damage not only to your children but also to your marriage. Because God created men to be the head of the home, any discord a father promotes will have lasting ripple effects.

Another way a father can bring disunity into the home is in discipline. I remember visiting with a family once that asked me to counsel them through a minor marital issue. As we began talking in their living room, their 5-year-old daughter repeatedly interrupted. I have to admit I was getting quite frustrated as the child was obviously seeking to be the center of attention, making any attempt at counseling impossible. What made matters worse, however, was that every time the wife tried to discipline the child for interrupting, the father would undercut his wife by saying, "Honey, she's fine." Although this may have seemed minor at that moment, it was clear this child learned that she had the ability to divide and conquer, reducing the consequences of her poor behavior. The wife, on the other hand, was left feeling disrespected and foolish not only in front of me but also with her daughter. Fathers, because God made us the head of the home, it is our responsibility to cultivate a spirit of unity within the home. There may be times when you and your spouse disagree over discipline, but never debate this in front of your children. If you disagree on a particular punishment, honor your wife publicly and then discuss the matter in private away from your children. Openly undermining your wife's discipline in front of others only works to divide not only your household but also your wife's heart.

Vision

Leaders set the course, the pace, and the emotional temperature for their teams. What makes a leader great is that they know where they are headed and they can inspire people to follow. When it comes to family, God has ordained fathers to be the visionary leaders within the home. Proverbs 29:18 says, "Where there is no prophetic vision the people cast off restraint, but blessed is he who keeps the law." This proverb is often quoted at deacon meetings, business luncheons, and at the kick-off of fundraising campaigns. Yet, when you read this proverb in its context, you will notice that the preceding verses emphasize parental responsibility to discipline children for godliness. "The rod and the reproof give wisdom, but a child left to himself brings shame to his mother" (Proverbs 29:15). "Discipline your son, and he will give you rest; he will give delight to your heart" (Proverbs 29:17). The vision fathers are to set for their families is one of faithful obedience to God's laws.

Sadly, many men fail not only in setting vision for godly living, but they fail in setting a vision for the future altogether. One of the greatest tragedies of our day is that many Christian fathers have not taken the time to cast a compelling vision for their families. Subsequently, many children meander through adolescence and college, piling up debt with no direction at all. Wives often end up feeling disoriented and confused when children are no longer in the home to be cared for. As the leader of the home, it is a husband's role not only to set the direction for your family but also to lead out in executing this vision. One practical way dads can cast a vision for their family is by developing a family vision statement. Think about some of the great vision statements you have seen in the business world:

- "Our vision is to be earth's most customer-centric company; to build a place where people can come to find and discover anything they might want to buy online." (Amazon)
- "We believe that we are on the face of the earth to make great products and that's not changing." (Apple)
- "To bring inspiration and innovation to every athlete in the world." (Nike)

A family vision statement will not only help to organize your family's focus, but also create a sense of destiny within your home. Everyone under your roof will know exactly whom they belong to, what is expected of them as members, and what your family represents in the world. Furthermore, not only will your immediate household have clarity, but also those visiting under your roof will clearly know what the ethos of your home is. Visitors entering your home will quickly get a feel for what kinds of behaviors, language, and conversations are acceptable within your home. For instance, our family vision statement reads like this:

> "Hate Sin, Love the Church, Marry a Good Woman"

As you can imagine, the words "Hate Sin" send a message to all who walk into our kitchen. The words "Love the Church" keep my sons (pastor's kids!) grounded in the mission that God has called our family to when the going gets tough. Finally, the words "Marry a Good Woman" have provided countless conversations about Christian character and the attributes that God values. In a culture where boys and girls are taught to objectify one another, this statement has offered our family repeated opportunities to teach our sons the qualities they should be looking for in their future spouses.

Fathers, leadership is tough, no doubt about it. There is a weight that comes when we realize that we form our children's view of God as Father. Yet, 2 Timothy 1:7 says, "For God gave us a spirit not of fear but of power and love and self-control." We are living in an age where evil is called good and good is called evil, not unlike that of 1st Century Corinthians. Yet, it was in this sin-infested culture where Paul writes these words of admonishment to the church: "For though you have countless guides in Christ, you do not have many fathers. For I became your father in Christ Jesus through the gospel. I urge you, then, be imitators of me" (1 Corinthians 4:15-16). Dads, providing an example worthy of imitation does not mean you need to be perfect, so drop that weight! To be worthy of imitation simply means to work hard at living out the gospel in front of your children. Demonstrate repentance in front of your children when you sin against them or your spouse. Speak of your need for greater faith to live as a sacrificial servant. Give daily reminders to your family that the cross paid for your sins and the resurrection gives us hope. Finally, dads, model a personal prayer life for your children. There is no greater way to lead your family than to have them walk in on you and catch you on your knees. Dads, find a place in your home where you go to pray regularly, and let your wife and kids walk in on you while you are praying. The vision you seared in their minds is one of complete dependence on God. Leadership is tough; so, men, show your family you are weak by getting on your knees in prayer.

SHE SAID

The ER doctor's words are seared into my conscience. "Why didn't you come sooner? We could have stopped this from happening."

I had been having contractions for 24 hours, but I was under the false impression that it was just common pregnancy discomfort for a woman carrying twins. It wasn't until my water broke that I came to my senses. I was about to deliver twins – much too early. I woke Dan up and called my doctor who told us to go immediately to the hospital. However, it was not the hospital I was pre-registered at; it was the one that had the best neonatal intensive care unit.

When we arrived, a nurse brought me back immediately and attached some type of contraction measuring machine to my belly. She watched the reading, gasped, and stared at me as if I had lost my mind.

"Don't you *feel* that? Those are big contractions."

"I . . . I thought it was just a bad night. I didn't know I was in labor . . . I didn't know."

"There's no turning back now."

That's when the ER doctor walked in and said those awful, guilt-inducing words to me . . . *Why didn't you come sooner? We could have stopped this from happening.* But it was too late. The babies were on their way, and the intensive care unit was waiting for them.

When they were born, I didn't get a chance to hold my babies, kiss them, feed them, or even take a good look at them. As soon as they were delivered, they were rushed out of the room to the waiting team. Later that night, Dan and I were allowed to visit them for the first time. We identified them from across the room by the names written on the incubators: "Trippie Boy A" and "Trippie Boy B."

Dan pushed my wheelchair towards them slowly, afraid of what we might see. They were so tiny, so beautiful, and so helpless. There were IVs on every inch of their little bodies, taped to their translucent skin and on their scalps, feeding tubes in their nose, monitors, and machines . . . all too much to take in. We couldn't hold them, but we were allowed to put our hands inside the incubators and touch them. I vividly remember the way Dan gently laid his hand on Dominick, and his hand was bigger than Dominick's whole body.

The prognosis wasn't good. They both had critical heart and lung problems. The list of severe problems that could arise in the future due to their prematurity was too much to take in. No one could tell us when and if they would come home.

If only I had called sooner. They could have been born as healthy, strong babies. I could have held them, fed them, and taken them home a day or two later. But that was not the story that God had written for us. I didn't understand it, nor did I like it. These babies did not deserve such suffering because of my ignorance. Did they?

Guilt

I sank into my darkest moment a couple days after my babies were born. When the monitors suddenly began screaming, a nurse came running over to my son. She pushed me away and called for help while performing CPR on his tiny body. Sam's heart had stopped beating. As his mother, I was merely the one who was pushed aside, unable to help my own child. I had no control over his life, whether his heart stopped beating again or whether he took another breath. I was helpless and sunk into a pit of guilt and despair. If only I had known better; if only I had called sooner . . . if only. I could not be enough, do enough, or give enough to save my child's life. The guilt was consuming me, and I was unraveling.

This guilt — it plagues us as mothers. It is this almost constant struggle with feelings of failure and inadequacy. Guilt inducing triggers can fall anywhere on the spectrum of motherhood from the health of our child to the designer of our child's jeans. It is because of *my* ignorance that my child is on life support. It is because of *my* low income that *I* can't provide the best clothes for my child. It is because of *my* poor disciplinary techniques that my child is throwing a tantrum in the Target check-out line. The list of triggers is inexhaustible, and I am exhausted.

This exhaustion that comes from striving to keep up and from feelings of failure resulting in guilt will damage our marriage and our children. Sooner or later, moms, we all come to the realization that we are not God, and if we continue to try to be Him by attempting to provide for every need and control every circumstance, we will fail miserably. The recognition of this truth is a start. Where we take our struggles, pride, guilt, and exhaustion is where true change of heart can take place. Moms, we need to take them to Christ on the cross, where he paid the ultimate price for our sins and exchanged them for righteousness. At the cross, we can find freedom from guilt because of the costly grace of Jesus. At the cross, there is freedom from feeling like my child's existence, health, and happiness are dependent on my capabilities as his or her mother. Christ's work on the cross is enough to bear away our guilt and shame and sustain us through each and every struggle on the spectrum of motherhood. "There is therefore now no condemnation for those who are in Christ Jesus" (Romans 8:1).

Model

I want my children to know this freedom that is available in Christ. Therefore, it is my privilege and responsibility to teach my children the gospel. Those who love God themselves should do what they can to engage the affections of their children to Him.[2]

> You shall love the Lord your God with all your heart and with all your soul and with all your might. And these words that I command you today shall be on your heart. You shall teach them diligently to your children, and shall talk of them when you sit in your house, and when you walk by the way, and when you lie down, and when you rise. You shall bind them as a sign on your hand, and they shall be as frontlets between your eyes. You shall write them on the doorposts of your house and on your gates. (Deuteronomy 6:5-9)

We should seek to model the gospel in our daily lives to our children. They must see us aware of our constant need for and reliance on God, living lives of repentance and forgiveness, and pursuing intimacy with Him - teaching in word, modeling in deed. "Therefore be imitators of God, as beloved children. And walk in love, as Christ loved us and gave himself up for us" (Ephesians 5:1,2a).

As a wife and mother, much of my responsibility lies in building the spiritual environment in our home. Is our home a respite and place of peace in the midst of an ungodly and chaotic world? Do my children see me studying the Word and praying daily? Am I showing them unconditional love, forgiving and extending grace as Christ does for me? Would they consider me to be emotionally stable, or do they wonder when I'm going to lose my temper and lash out? There are many considerations when building the spiritual environment in your home, but I believe the most powerful model of the gospel in the home is the marriage.

Wives, we have the privilege of teaching our children the gospel by respecting and submitting to our husband as we reflect the Trinity. When our children see us repent to our husband when we sin, and forgive our husband when he sins against us, we are modeling a Christ-like relationship to them. By showing affection to my husband and joy when we are together, our children are filled with a peace and confidence that everything is going to be all right because mom and dad love each other unconditionally as Christ loves us. The marriage that your children see in your home will provide the vision for their future marriages. What do you hope for in your child's marriage?

Discipline

I am asked almost as many questions about disciplining a child as I am about marriage. Look at it this way with me: the discipline of a child, or lack of it, can have tremendous implications on your marriage. Marriage and the training of children go hand-in-hand. Ephesians 6:4 commands us to bring our children up in the discipline and instruction of the Lord. As parents, we have a God-given authority in our children's lives as we act on His behalf in the discipline and instruction of our children. Let's look at some practical ways to build the marriage while living out our duty to discipline our children.

Unite and Conquer

The marriage is the most important relationship in the home, taking priority over the parent/child relationship. As I stated earlier, generally speaking, when mom and dad are doing well in marriage, the children are content. However, if the children suddenly seem uncharacteristically disobedient or anxious, first, look at your marriage. Is there unresolved conflict creating tension in your home? Are mom and dad doing well, but the family schedule is out of control creating stress in the home? Has mom or dad been away from home more than usual creating unease among the children? Often, the behavior of the children is in correlation to the intimacy between mom and dad.

When it comes to discipline, parents must be unified. Your children need to see that mom and dad are in love *and* in agreement. If mom says "no," the children should not even think of going to dad for a different answer, knowing that mom and dad will be in agreement.

Teach Obedience

Every time a parent takes the time to teach obedience, he or she is using an opportunity to teach the gospel. To discipline disobedience is a part of teaching children that they should obey a Father who judges impartially but provides a ransom through Christ[3] (1 Peter 1:14-21).

Children need to know the importance of immediate obedience. Counting to 10 or giving 3 strikes are not useful strategies in teaching children obedience. Because God will not be annoyed or ignored, neither should parents. No children should feel the freedom to ignore a parent's direction, nor should they feel like the parent's discipline is motivated by personal annoyance. Parents must ask for grace to deal patiently with sin. But deal with it we must.[4] Allowing children to disobey their parent's command will be allowing them to disobey God's command.

Dig Deep

While it is important to immediately address the outward behavior, it is a temporary solution to a much bigger issue: the sinful heart. The heart determines the behavior (Mark 7:21).

I barely survived parenting twin boys during those early childhood years. The discipline seemed never-ending, and sometimes I just wanted to take the easy way out of a stressful or embarrassing situation rather than take the time and emotional energy to deal with the heart of the matter. You know what I mean – using candy as bribery, pretending to not see the smaller acts of defiance, removing myself from a situation so I do not have to deal with it, and more candy. However, God is nowhere near concerned with our outward behavior as He is with our heart. As tired as we parents may be, we must address it.

According to Tedd Tripp, addressing the heart means helping our children understand themselves, God's ways, sin, and the saving gospel of Jesus Christ. It also includes helping them understand their motivations, desires, and goals while encouraging faith in Jesus Christ. The only way to address the heart is through deep, meaningful, biblical communication.[5] Ask the right questions. Listen intently. Speak wisely. Pray. Forgive. These practices, mom and dad, will also grow intimacy in your marriage.

Give Grace

Let's be realistic. We're not perfect, and neither are our sweet little children. Our goal in discipline is not perfect obedience or behavior; it is to teach them that sin has consequences, and that we all need the saving grace of Jesus Christ. It is to teach them that sinners who come to Jesus in repentance and faith will find forgiveness and mercy. Mom and dad, that goes for all of us. God's gracious love desires to rid me and you and all our children of the sins that keep us from him. Let us remember the cross daily, reminding our children that we are sinners just like them, and then point them to the grace of Christ.

Give your children grace. Give your husband grace. Show how Jesus continues to redeem your marriage and your family because of His saving grace.

GOD SAID

If you have children, it is because God chose to reward you with them. Psalm 127:3 states, "Behold, children are a heritage from the Lord, the fruit of the womb a reward." We have the opportunity, as parents, to image our Heavenly Father to our children.

Being a parent can be one of the most joyful experiences that married couples share. It can be heartwarming, hilarious, and exasperating all in one day. We have had many moments when our boys made us laugh until we cried or left us in awe of God's goodness because of their kindness. However, our children have a sin nature, as do all children.

In many ways, the attitude or disposition of the children sets the ethos, or spirit, of the home. Happy children make for a happy home; angry children make for an angry home; stressed-out children make for a stressed-out home. Although this may be a reality, it is not the way God has designed the home. The spirit of the home is to fall squarely on the parents. Unfortunately, over the last 50 years or so, the marketing world has spent millions of dollars targeting our children and inundating them with choices. Children choose the restaurant to eat lunch at, the family vacation spot, and whether the family will go to church or not. After all of this, subtly, we can believe that it is our role as their parents to keep them happy. However, the danger of appeasing our children is that we risk damaging our marriage and inverting God's created order.

Parents, remember that you have the God-given authority over the children and the home, and you have been given that authority as a unified team. Your marriage – not your children – should set the ethos of the home. A unified marriage is the best gift parents can give their children.

Your marriage can survive parenting. Better yet, when parenting God's way, your marriage can thrive.

YOU SAID

1) How are we doing in imaging our Heavenly Father as we are parenting?
2) What are some ways in which you can become more unified in the area of discipline? Are there any areas of disagreement that need to be worked out?
3) Together, strategize a plan for discipline that prioritizes addressing the heart. What are some patterns of sin that you see in your child? How can you get to the heart of the issue with him or her?
4) Is there any mom or dad guilt that you need to take to the cross?
5) Take some time to talk and pray about your family vision. Write out a family motto.

HOW CAN
WE HAVE AN
ENDURING
MARRIAGE?

CHAPTER 6

HOW CAN WE HAVE AN ENDURING MARRIAGE?

HE SAID

It was spectacular and sad at the same time. At the age of 80 you could still hear pet names used, catch hands being held, and if you looked quick you might even catch a peck on the lips. Sure, there was an occasional snap of the tongue like elderly are prone to, but it was quickly met with the wink of an eye. Daryl and Lucille loved each other. After 60 years of marriage they still laughed and enjoyed one another's company. The day Lucille was laid to rest was the day all 6'3" of Daryl crumbled under the weight of love. We knew it would not be long before he joined her.

It was perhaps the saddest thing Gina and I had ever seen, yet it was completely glorious. We were 7 years into our marriage, still learning each other while navigating toddling twins. The urgency of the immediate seemed to consume all our thoughts. Diapers, doctors, bills, it all seemed so crushing. The pace of life in those days made it hard to see past the next feeding and nap time. Yet, when Gina's grandparents passed away, they provided for us something many never get to witness. An example of a marriage that finished well!

Models

The mysterious law of the human soul is that we imitate what we esteem. God has hard-wired all of us intuitively for imitation. As image bearers, we are designed to replicate what we admire. For this reason we all need examples of marriages that we respect. Unfortunately, with current divorce rates near 50%, it is increasingly difficult to find examples of compelling marriages.[1] Not only has divorce made it difficult to find enduring marriages, but the worship wars of the last 20 years have damaged church unity in profound ways. The battle over "traditional" services vs. "contemporary" services has resulted in separated congregations where younger people and older people no longer worship together. This new form of segregation has left our churches void of older marriages to model. More than ever we need to see reconciliation between elderly and youthful congregations. The elderly of our churches serve a vital role that cannot be replaced. Elderly married couples give to younger couples a vision of hope!

At every stage of our marriage, we face new territory. As I write this, I am navigating the waters of middle life. To date I have not bought a Harley Davidson (not ruling it out) or gone sky diving (completely ruling that out), but I am thinking a lot about what comes next in life. What can Gina and I expect as 45-year-old empty nesters? How do we parent adult children? How do we handle physical changes that are naturally occurring? We all need someone a few seasons ahead to lead the way for us. Thankfully, God has brought us some older couples who are coaching us through this time. Men, we need to ruthlessly seek out married couples that are at least one to two seasons ahead of us in life and marriage. Once you find these couples, you and your wife would do well to submit to their counsel. My suggestion would be that this couple not be your parents. You will always be your parents' child, and no matter how old you are it will be difficult for them to lead with un-bias eyes.

As you seek this out, look for a couple that never speaks ill of each other, a couple that appears lighthearted when in each other's company, and a couple that still holds hands in church. In short, find a marriage that you and your wife find compelling, and let them lead you into the next seasons of life.

Motivation

Anyone who knows me quickly learns that I love the Rocky movies. If you never have seen a Rocky movie, first repent, then go to your nearest movie rental store and rent all 6 of them. Rocky is a powerful story of an underdog boxer who becomes the heavyweight champion of the world. In every movie, Rocky is against unbeatable odds where nobody believes in him. Nobody, that is, except his wife Adrianne. When people think of the Rocky movies seldom are they thinking love story, but that is exactly what makes Rocky resonate with men. Every man feels somewhat like an underdog in his own right. To some degree, every man is trying to prove that he is worthy of respect. At one point in the first movie, just before Rocky is going to fight the heavyweight champ, Apollo Creed, he whispers to Adrianne, "It really don't matter if I lose this fight. It really don't matter if this guy opens my head, either. 'Cause all I wanna do is go the distance. Nobody's ever gone the distance with Creed, and if I can go that distance, you see, and that bell rings and I'm still standin', I'm gonna know for the first time in my life, see, that I weren't just another bum from the neighborhood."

Deep in every man's heart he wants to prove to a woman that he is not just another bum from the neighborhood. The fascinating irony of Rocky, however, is that Adrianne never sees him this way. Win or lose, she always believes in him and respects him. What makes the Rocky movies so inspiring is that Rocky's drive to succeed comes because there is a woman who believes in him. In addition to finding older mentors for marriage, I would also suggest finding stories that motivate you to finish well in your marriage.

George and Mary Müller are an example of a motivating marriage story. They married October 7th, 1830.[2] From the onset of their nuptials, the couple abandoned any idea of saving money or putting aside for their future. Both George and Mary willfully decided at the beginning of their marriage to live purely on faith, trusting in the Lord to provide all their needs. The couple reduced their expenses and simplified life in such a way that they could give away the maximum about of money possible. Through the course of their life the couple cared for over 10,000 orphans and saw upwards of £1,381,171 (approximately $2,718,844 US) pass through their hands without soliciting a single donation. The faith of this couple is truly uplifting, but what might be more inspiring is the love that grew between the two in the midst of such a taxing ministry. When Mary Müller passed away February 6th, 1870, after 40 years of marriage, her husband George fell to his knees and praised God for giving him such a helpful and supportive wife. At her funeral 5 days later, these are the words Müller spoke:

> Were we happy? Verily we were. With every year our happiness increased more and more. I never saw my beloved wife at any time, when I met her unexpectedly anywhere in Bristol, without being delighted so to do. I never met her even in the Orphan Houses, without my heart being delighted so to do. Day by day, as we met in our dressing room, at the Orphan Houses, to wash our hands before dinner and tea, I was delighted to meet her, and she was equally pleased to see

me. Thousands of times I told her - "My darling,
I never saw you at any time, since you became my
wife, without my being delighted to see you."[3]

George and Mary endured the pain of delivering two
stillborn children. They felt the pressure of financial burdens
resulting from their decision to keep no material wealth. The
couple knew the stress of thousands of children depending
on them for guidance and discipline. Yet at the end of their
marriage, the legacy left was a couple who loved each other
deeply.

Another motivating marriage from this era is that
of Charles and Susannah Spurgeon. At the time of their
meeting, Charles Spurgeon was soaring to heights of fame as
an eloquent nineteen-year-old preacher. Susannah Thompson
was admittedly unimpressed by his oratory skills. Yet, Miss
Thompson grew under Spurgeon's preaching and became
awakened to her spiritual condition. On April 20th, 1854
Charles gave to young Susannah an illustrated copy of John
Bunyan's *Pilgrim's Progress* with the following inscription,
"Miss Thompson, with desires for her progress in the blessed
pilgrimage, from C. H. Spurgeon." It was Spurgeon's pure
concern for Susannah's spiritual condition that ignited a love
between the two. Susannah later wrote in her journal the
following in response to the gift she received:

> I do not think, that my beloved had at that
> time any other thought concerning me than to
> help a struggling soul Heavenward; but I was
> greatly impressed by his concern for me, and the
> book became very precious as well as helpful.
> By degrees, though with much trembling, I told
> him of my state before God and he gently led
> me, by his preaching, and by his conversations,
> through the power of the Holy Spirit to the cross

of Christ for the peace and pardon my weary soul
was longing for.

The couple was married January 8th, 1856 and began
their years of ministry together. Spurgeon's fame continued
to grow, keeping him away from home oftentimes for weeks
on end. Yet, Susannah did not grow bitter. She knew God
was using her husband mightily, and she was willing to die
to her own wants and desires in order to serve the Lord. On
September 20th, 1856, before their first wedding anniversary,
Susannah gave birth to twin boys, Charles and Thomas. The
delivery was strenuous on Susannah's body, however, and the
remainder of her life would be lived out in weakness, battling
various physical ailments. Charles Spurgeon would spend
the next 30 years loving his wife and caring for her in her
frailty until his death in 1892. It is estimated that Spurgeon
preached to upwards of 10,000,000 people during the course
of his ministry, all the while battling severe depression of his
own.[4] With such a strenuous and pressure-filled schedule, one
might wonder what the home life was like for the Spurgeons.
The following excerpt from Susannah's diary sheds light on
the relationship between the couple. Several years after her
husband's death, Susannah wrote the following:

> Ah! My husband, the blessed earthly ties which
> we welcomed so rapturously are dissolved now,
> and death has hidden thee from my mortal eyes;
> but not even death can divide thee from me or
> sever the love which united our hearts so closely.
> I feel it living and growing still, and I believe it
> will find its full and spiritual development only
> when we shall meet in the glory-land and worship
> together before the throne!

After years of physical and emotional pain, Charles and
Susannah finished well. Though their marriage was filled

with troubles and trials, the Spurgeons lived motivated by the glory of God to endure and leave a legacy that images Christ's endurance with his people. It is important not only that married couples find mentors for coaching, but also that we find marriage stories that motivate husbands and wives to finish well.

Mission

In recent years a new buzzword has emerged among evangelical Christians. That word is *missional*. Although many have used this word to mean different things, the concept is really quite simple. The fundamental notion behind the word missional is that Christians are to live their lives in and among unbelievers for the purpose of proclaiming the good news of Jesus Christ. Missiologist Dwight Smith says it this way, "What God is going to do in the world, he will do using all his people." The great commission calls believers to proclaim the goodness of God while living in the normalcy of life. One of the most powerful ways Christians can live out the call to mission is to have compelling marriages on display for an unbelieving world to examine.

I have never sat with a young couple in premarital counseling who hopes for their marriage to fail. Never have I had a couple say to me, "Our dream is to be divorced after five years." At no time has anyone ever said to me, "Our vision for the future is a custody battle where we get to see our children every other week." Every couple, whether they call themselves Christian or not, wants to succeed. Every couple goes into marriage desiring to live happily ever after. We may differ with skeptics of Christianity over evolution, the virgin birth, and even the resurrection of Christ. But one area where we find common ground is man's universal desire for lasting relationship. For this reason, Christian marriage becomes a powerful missional activity where believing couples can find common ground to engage the culture.

Christianity is the only worldview that ensures genuine believing couples will last. The gospel is the good news that Jesus died to take the punishment for our sins and the sins committed against us. When husbands and wives truly believe this, they no longer will need to punish one another for the sins they commit against each other. When Jesus became our sacrificial substitute, husbands and wives were given the freedom to forgive one another just as Christ forgives. Not only does the gospel give us the freedom to forgive, but Jesus promises to send the Holy Spirit, empowering us to forgive. In the hours before Jesus went to the cross he told his disciples, "If you love me, you will keep my commandments. And I will ask the Father, and he will give you another Helper, to be with you forever, even the Spirit of truth, whom the world cannot receive, because it neither sees him nor knows him. You know him, for he dwells with you and will be in you" (John 14:15-17).

Of all the world religions, only Christianity provides a way to deal with marital offenses justly. In the cross, divine justice was served, and in the cross heavenly grace was extended. When I spend time talking to couples who have suffered the pain of divorce, I find more often than not it was years of unforgivness, bitterness and resentment that finally destroyed their union. Only the cross of Jesus offers a solution to these and other marriage killers. When couples will commit to live their marriage in light of the cross, a bond of love flows which is supremely supernatural. Unbelieving couples who are given access into a genuine Christian marriage will find a uniqueness that begs the question, "What makes your marriage so different?" In a world that denigrates, belittles, and treats marriage as passé, Christian marriage has the opportunity to stand out as something uniquely other.

Have you ever considered perhaps the most missional activity you and your spouse can engage in is living happily ever after? The reason so many stories end this way is all humans desire to make it to the end of life loving someone and being loved. Now more than ever, Christian couples need to realize unbelieving friends and family members are watching to see if your faith affects the real things in life, things like your marriage.

We were double dating with a couple from our church just nine months after their wedding. I was privileged to perform the ceremony, so I was even more eager to hear how married life was going. As we pulled up to the table in the dimly lit coffee shop, we noticed the young girl sitting next to us was quite intrigued by our conversation. She was eavesdropping on our every word, leaning in like she had a 3-foot musky on the line. Finally, when the awkwardness became quite uncomfortable, she stood up and approached our table. "Forgive me, but I have been listening to you and I am completely bewildered about your topic. For the life of me, I can't understand why anyone in this day and age would still participate in an institution like marriage. Do you mind if I join in on your conversation?" Wow, I thought, this kind of thing only happens to Billy Graham! "Well," I said, "would you mind if I told you a story?" "Not at all," the young woman replied. The next 2 hours were consumed retelling the story of an unfaithful spouse and a persistent lover. We talked about a spouse who unconditionally loved even when his love was rejected. We recounted the courage of a husband who sacrificed even when his love was spurned. We painted a picture of a lover who would never leave, always do good, and never be unfaithful. As we completed the story, we shared about a wedding feast where the bride and the groom will celebrate a unity that can never be broken. As we came to the conclusion of the story, tears flowed down her face as I gently asked, "Wouldn't it be nice to have a spouse like this?" "Yes, yes it would," she replied.

SHE SAID

A few summers ago we were given the very generous gift of a boat. We are a family who loves to fish and swim and go tubing. Okay, I don't like to go tubing, but my three guys do, so that's nice for them. I am content to take pictures while attempting to decipher their hand signals from the boat. (*I think he's saying slow down. No, maybe he means speed up. What does the right arm flailing in the air mean again? Stop! Man down!*) Here is the best part of tubing though: the unadulterated joy on my sons' faces. Dan and I call it the preschool laugh. It is pure, innocent and uninhibited laughter that you rarely see from a teenager and never see from an adult. And when they laugh like that, I am immediately drawn back to those early childhood years, when innocence permeated our home, filling it with seemingly constant joyful noise. Any mother of grown children will tell you how fast time moves, and this year, for me personally, this truth is becoming more and more real.

This is the year that our sons began high school. Yesterday they were in preschool, and tomorrow they will be off to college. It is likely that Dan and I will be 45-year-old empty nesters. That's the thing about having twins – our oldest and youngest children will leave home at the same time. As I consider them leaving, a flood of emotions threatens to overwhelm me. But I don't have to dig too deep to find a twinge of excitement about what God may have planned for Dan and I. We are soon going to experience marriage, as it was when it began – without kids at home to care for, spending more time enjoying each other.

This is Good

As this change in our married life seems more and more imminent, I am reminded of this truth: the season of life with children at home is relatively temporary (only 18 years or so), but the marriage is not. I understand the wisdom of God's created order of human relationships that places the marriage before any other. And as I anticipate this next season of our marriage, I rest in the truth that God's plans for us and our children are good.

I know that His plans are good because God is good (Luke 18:19) and He is the source of everything good (James 1:17). We, as God's creation, would be nonexistent without His provision. He is the Giver; we are the recipients. And this is a good thing, because His plans are way better than any we could imagine.

Wives, as the recipients of God's gifts, we must believe that our husband was given to us for our good. God has lovingly and sovereignly chosen our husband for us! We must receive our husband as the gift that he is so that we may grow to reflect God's image.

Receiving your husband is much more than just accepting him. It means embracing the God-given differences that He has built into each one of you.[5] If there ever is a time when you question the choice that you made when marrying your husband, trust the sovereignty of God. He can do all things, and no purpose of His can be thwarted (Job 42:2). If there ever is a time when your marriage seems hopeless, remember: God will give good things to those who ask him (Matthew 7:11). His desire is for His children to have fruitful, enduring marriages. Ask Him for that. Trust in the plans God has for you, and embrace the desires He has for you and your marriage. They are good, and God is pleased when you enjoy His gifts.

For you, O Lord, are my hope, my trust, O Lord,
from my youth. (Psalm 71:5)

Enjoy your Husband

It was 1989 and my friend Stacy had a crush on a boy in our youth group named Dan. As our youth group planned a formal banquet, Stacy convinced me to attempt a set-up between her and Dan so that he would ask her to the banquet. I figured I had nothing to lose and walked confidently up to Dan and said, "Would you like to take Stacy to the banquet?" His reply, "No, but I'd like to take you."

Can you guess my response? It was nothing short of throwing Stacy under the bus and accepting his invitation. That was the end of my short-lived friendship with Stacy, but the beginning of a lifelong friendship with Dan. He is my best friend.

This is my beloved and this is my friend. (Song
of Solomon 5:16)

I am thankful beyond measure for the gift of a best friend who knows me, loves me, and makes me laugh on a daily basis. Dan has many qualities, but his sense of humor is one of my favorites.

As Proverbs tells us, a joyful heart is good medicine (17:22), but humor brings more than physiological benefits to a husband and wife. Humor helps us build an enduring friendship. Husbands and wives who want their marriages to be enduring and endearing must be friends.[6] Have some fun together! Remember back to the early days of dating and marriage before children. What are some of your favorite memories, special dates, or funniest moments? Think of some creative ways to grow your friendship and enjoy your husband. Can you imagine how pleasing it is to God to see his children enjoying the gift of marriage?

Have Fun

Admittedly, there are many activities or dates that Dan would prefer more than I would. But one way I can show him love and enjoy his friendship is by joining him in some of his favorite activities. Let's take fishing, for example. I'm no amateur when it comes to fishing, let me tell you. I am grateful for a dad that took the time to teach his little girl how to put a worm on a hook and snag a fish. And this life lesson proves to be beneficial to my marriage, especially since we received the boat. Dan loves to fish. If he could spend all of his free time "throwing out a few lines," I believe he would. A couple years ago, I enrolled in a free Fly Fishing course at a local store. (You can call it an investment into my marriage). Is Fly Fishing my favorite activity? Um, no. But is spending time with Dan? Oh, yes. On those days when Buffalo weather prevents us from fishing off our boat, there's always Fly Fishing. And a happy husband.

What are your favorite activities to do together? I asked several wives to give me their creative and practical ideas for having fun and building an enduring friendship with their husband. Here are some of their responses:

- Several years ago we axed cable. Finding something to do that's not staring at a talking box after the kids go to bed forces creativity and conversation.
- Good old-fashioned board games are very underrated.
- We go to bed at the same time and have lots of pillow talk.
- We enjoy cooking and baking together – and we do the grocery shopping together first.
- I'm his biggest cheerleader, literally. When he runs his marathons or plays in football games, I'm always on the sidelines cheering him on.

- We love to window shop for furniture together, to plan what our future home will look like.
- Every night at bedtime, we hold hands and walk upstairs together.
- My husband loves to hike, so we take trips to the Adirondacks together. It is rewarding because it makes my husband happy and is good for our health at the same time.
- We have 1 hour of "couch time" every night, and discussion about the weather or our jobs is banned from the couch.
- Most of our date nights happen when the kids go to bed. We love to cook creative snacks for that time. Last night it was chocolate-covered popcorn!
- I watch his favorite TV shows and football games with him.
- We protect date night. No grocery shopping or errands allowed on dates.
- We go to church together.
- Laugh a lot!
- Walk the beach and talk about our day.
- NEVER go to bed mad!
- Make sure we see or talk to our children and grandchildren as often as possible.
- Never say hurtful things to each other.
- Sit quietly together and read books.
- Sometimes I get involved in outdoor activities with him, but he is just as happy if I am there watching and cheering him on in flag football, ultimate frisbee, etc.
- I take an interest in things that are important to him – even politics!
- The two of us do fun and goofy things together that most adults wouldn't do without their children, like mini-golf, amusement and water parks, roller skating and bowling.

Back to the Beginning

In closing, let us glance back to scripture quoted in Chapter 1. We read about the creation of the first wife in Genesis 2:18: "Then the Lord God said, 'It is not good that the man should be alone; I will make him a helper fit for him.'"

Remember, this was the first time in creation that God deemed something "not good." It was not good that Adam was alone because he did not have a woman to walk alongside of him as his partner, lover and friend. God's solution to this was a friendship in the covenant of marriage.[7] God gave Adam a wife . . . a friend for life. And God in his sovereign goodness has chosen you to be the only wife your husband's got. Your marriage is a beautiful gift. Embrace, nurture, celebrate and enjoy it!

> May the God of endurance and encouragement grant you to live in such harmony with one another, in accord with Christ Jesus, that together you may with one voice glorify the God and Father of our Lord Jesus Christ. (Romans 15:5,6)

GOD SAID

Making it to the end is easy to talk about and hard to do. As married couples, we must be determined to endure. While this may seem daunting as we consider the difficult and sanctifying work ahead of each of us in our marriage, we can rest in the promises of God. Philippians 1:6: And I am sure of this, that he who began a good work in you will bring it to completion at the day of Jesus Christ.

Obviously, Gina and I have yet to make it until the end together, but we are hopeful that if we take God at His word and trust in His promises, He will deliver us safely home. For marriages that endure until the end, we must determine to forgive one another as Christ has forgiven us, to sacrifice for one another as Christ sacrificed for us, and finally, to enjoy one another as Christ enjoys us.

YOU SAID

1) Name 5 marriages that you would consider to be compelling, and discuss what makes them different.
2) What married couple could serve as a mentor to you?
3) Talk about your funniest early memories together.
4) Come up with 3 creative activities to do together that will build your friendship. Schedule them into your calendar in the next month.
5) What couple can you open your life to for the purpose of sharing the gospel?

EPILOGUE

HE SAID

When Gina and I got married, we didn't know what we didn't know. I was 22 years old on our wedding day and Gina was 21. We were immature, foolish, and truly believed the world owed us something. After all, we were high school sweethearts and the world owed us happily ever after . . . or at least that's what we thought! Months into our marriage, reality hit us like a Brock Lesnar right hook. For this marriage to succeed, it needed help. In my naivety, I assumed if I just worked hard enough I could ensure happiness. After all, my limited experience taught me hard work was the key to success. The problem was the harder I worked, the angrier I became. I was working hard to provide, working hard to get ahead, and working hard to be loved. But the harder I worked, the more it seemed my marriage was slipping away. I had never failed at anything in my life; now, here I was standing on the edge of the biggest failure. I was about to lose the only girl I ever loved! For this marriage to succeed, it needed help, but not the kind of help my hard work could provide. We needed the help of another.

It was October 1997 in a hotel room in Sarasota, Florida. Gina and I were hanging on by a sliver when we attended my best friend's wedding. When Jeff asked me to be his best man, tidal waves of guilt washed over me. "How can I stand up and offer a toast for my friend's marriage when my own is falling apart?" We left the rehearsal dinner that night feeling full of hope for our friends and sorry for ourselves. On the way back to the hotel room, I snuck away for my nightly drink and Marlboro Red. Gina retired to the room alone. She was used to it.

It was just after midnight when I crawled into bed, but little did I know I wouldn't sleep a wink. "I'm so alone, I'm so tired, I'm a failure," I thought to myself. Our marriage was over in my mind, and all our hope was now gone. I can remember how many hours passed before He arrived, but when He showed up, I knew exactly who it was. His presence was kind and His whisper was clear. It wasn't audible and it wasn't grandiose; it was just a thought . . . or maybe more like a whisper. "Come home," echoed in my soul, "Come home." Jesus came to me that night and offered me a way out of the mess I had created for myself. I prayed throughout the night, repeatedly telling him that I accepted his offer and believed his sacrifice was enough to forgive me. I never fell asleep that night; I didn't want to!

It was at a wedding where I finally surrendered my life to Jesus, and it was at a wedding where OUR restoration miracle began. I guess as I think about it, we shouldn't have been so surprised. Jesus has an affinity for wedding ceremonies!

SHE SAID

Dan and I had hopes and dreams for our "happily ever after" from the beginning of our courtship. I am sure that most married couples can relate to that, as we all go into marriage hoping for happiness and dreaming about growing old together. It wasn't too long before we messed it all up with our selfish agendas and disobedience to God's ways. A few months after we exchanged vows, our marriage began to destruct, and our happily ever after seemed more like an unrealistic fantasy.

However, that is not where our love story ended. God worked in our hearts as we grew in faithfulness to His word and trusted in His promises. It was then that God began to restore our marriage and give us a glimpse of what He desires to do in His Church, the Bride of Christ. Where we found hope for our marriage was in the greatest love story ever lived – Jesus paying our debt on the cross – for His undeserving and unfaithful Bride. Jesus is returning for her.

Our marriages are a preparation, a rehearsal of sorts, for the most incredible marriage that is to come. All of this work in marriage is simply about getting us, His Bride, ready for that big day – the day where we see Jesus, our Bridegroom, face-to-face, share a meal together, and celebrate our eternal union with Him.

Are you ready for *that* wedding?

'Let us rejoice and exult and give him the glory, for the marriage of the Lamb has come, and his Bride has made herself ready; it was granted her to clothe herself with fine linen, bright and pure' for the fine linen is the righteous deeds of the saints (Revelation 19:7-8).

NOTES

Chapter 1

1. John F. MacArthur, *Different by Design,* MacArthur Study Series (Wheaton, IL: Victor Books, 1996), 18.
2. Wendy Alsup, *The Gospel Centered Woman* (2012), 13.

Chapter 2

1. Kurt A. Richardson, vol. 36, James, The New American Commentary (Nashville: Broadman & Holman Publishers, 1997), 236.
2. Elyse Fitzpatrick, Helper by Design: God's Perfect Plan for *Women in Marriage* (Chicago, IL: Moody Publishers, 2003), 167.
3. Mark and Grace Driscoll, *Real Marriage: The Truth About Sex, Friendship & Life Together* (Nashville, TN: Thomas Nelson, 2012), 69.
4. Dave Harvey, *When Sinners Say "I Do": Discovering the Power of the Gospel for Marriage* (Wapwallopen, PA, 2007), 104.
5. Ibid., 103.

Chapter 3

1. Paul David Tripp, *Dangerous Calling: Confronting the Unique Challenges of Pastoral Ministry* (Wheaton, IL: Crossway, 2012), 163.
2. Matthew Henry's Commentary on the Whole Bible, New Modern Edition, electronic database (Peabody, MA: Hendrickson, 1991), comment on Mark 1:35.
3. Bob Deffinbaugh, "A Model for Marriage," *The Way of the Wise: Studies in the Book of Proverbs*, June 2, 2004, https://bible.org/seriespage/model-marriage.

Chapter 4

1. The Henry J. Kaiser Foundation, "Daily Media Use Among Children and Teens Up Dramatically From Five Years Ago," January 20, 2010, http://kff.org/disparities-policy/press-release/daily-media-use-among-children-and-teens-up-dramatically-from-five-years-ago/.
2. K. A. Mathews, vol. 1A, *Genesis 1-11:26*, The New American Commentary (Nashville: Broadman & Holman Publishers, 1996), 222.
3. Kevin Leman, Sex Begins in the Kitchen: Creating Intimacy to Make Your Marriage Sizzle, Grand Rapids, Michigan. Revell Publishing, 1981. pg 10.
4. Dave Harvey, *When Sinners Say "I Do": Discovering the Power of the Gospel for Marriage* (Wapwallopen, PA, 2007), 156.
5. Elyse Fitzpatrick, *Helper by Design: God's Perfect Plan for Women in Marriage* (Chicago, IL: Moody Publishers, 2003), 105.6.

Chapter 5

1. John F. MacArthur Jr., Alone with God, MacArthur Study Series (Wheaton, IL: Victor Books, 1995), 47.
2. Matthew Henry's Commentary on the Whole Bible, New Modern Edition, electronic database (Peabody, MA: Hendrickson, 1991), comment on Deuteronomy 6:5-9.
3. Jeremy Pierre, "Watch Your Conjunctions in Parenting," Feb. 1, 2012, http://thegospelcoalition.org/blogs/tgc/2012/02/01/watch-your-conjunctions-in-parenting.
4. Ibid.
5. Tedd Tripp, Shepherding a Child's Heart (Wapwallopen, PA: Shepherd Press, 1995), 90.

Chapter 6

1. Larry Frolick, "Why do people divorce?" Divorce Magazine, June 30, 2005, http://www.divorcemag.com/c/s3/?relationships/whydivorce*.
2. Steer, Rodger, George Müller, Delighted in God! (Wheaton, Illinois: Harold Shaw Publishers: 1975) 39.
3. Mueller, Narrative, 2:392-393.
4. http://www.iclnet.org/pub/resources/text/history/spurgeon/sp-bio.html
5. FamilyLife, The Art of Marriage, Getting to the Heart of God's Design, (Little Rock, AR: FamilyLife Publishing: 2012) 8.
6. Mark and Grace Driscoll, Real Marriage: The Truth About Sex, Friendship & Life Together (Nashville, TN: Thomas Nelson, 2012), 24.
7. Ibid., 37.

CPSIA information can be obtained at www.ICGtesting.com
Printed in the USA
BVOW04s1811310114

343542BV00001B/6/P